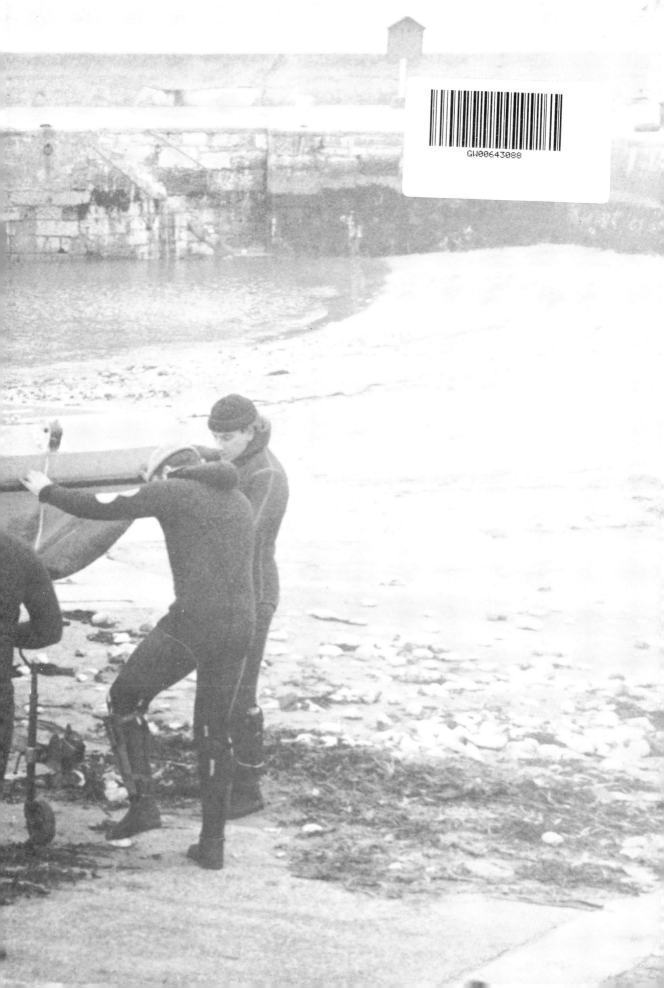

Ten Years Underwater

By Ned Middleton

IMMEL
Publishing

Phototypeset in Century Schoolbook,
by Datapage International Ltd., Dublin.

Printed in the Netherlands by Smeets Offset, BV, Weert.

Designed and Illustrated
by Larry Hynes, A&D (Galway).

IMMEL Publishing, Ely House, 37 Dover Street,
London W1X 3RB. Telephone: 01 491 1799.
Telex: UK 296582 (ELTOUP G) Fax: 01 409 1525

British Library Cataloguing in Publication Data

Middleton, Ned
Ten years underwater
1. Recreations. Underwater diving. Personal observations
I. Title
797.2/3/0924

ISBN 0-907151-43-4

Front Cover
● An aerial view of
the famous Blue Hole
of Belize. This is
the largest Blue Hole
in the world and the
only one, to my
knowledge, that is
large enough to take
a ship at anchor.

Other Sealife titles by IMMEL:
    Guide to Inshore Marine Life—David Erwin & Bernard Picton
    Sealife of Britain and Ireland—Edited by Elizabeth Wood
    Red Sea Invertebrates—Peter Vine
    Red Sea Reef Fishes—John E. Randall
    Diver's Guide to Red Sea Reef Fishes—John E. Randall
    Red Sea Safety—Peter Vine
    The Red Sea—Peter Vine
    Red Sea Explorers—Peter Vine & Hagen Schmid
    Sharks of Arabia—John E. Randall

CONTENTS

● Operation Raleigh.
Photo by author.

FOREWORD

By: The Earl of Lichfield

My job as a professional photographer takes me to the far corners of the globe and invariably brings me into contact with the sea and those people who earn their living from it. I have enjoyed listening to and reading the exploits of many divers with whom I have come into contact to the extent that I have now taken up the sport of Sub-Aqua Diving. "Ten Years Underwater", however, stands out because of the author's sheer enthusiasm and is a remarkably interesting and colourful account of his diving adventures in tropic and temperate seas. Some of the photographs are quite outstanding.

It is abundantly clear from reading these absorbing tales that neither a careful approach to the sport nor a restrained use of the marine environment need spoil one's enjoyment underwater.

I wish Ned Middleton well in his pursuit of new diving experiences and I sincerely hope we do not have to wait another ten years to read a sequel. . .

● Returning from a dive off 'Maggie's leap', Newcastle, Co. Down.

To Malcolm Newman
(1948–1984)
and divers like him

INTRODUCTION

Ned Middleton, British Army Captain and military accountant, has led a more active life than most men of his profession, serving both at home and abroad with such units as: The Special Air Service, The Gurkha Rifles, The Parachute Regiment, Royal Engineers, Royal Artillery, Army Air Corps, The Life Guards and his own corps, the Royal Army Pay Corps.

Some years ago, while living in Northern Ireland, he took up sports diving and within a year qualified as a British Sub-Aqua Club (BSAC) Instructor and a Joint Services Diving Supervisor. Since then, he has led numerous expeditions around the world and was privileged to become Chief Diver of Operation Raleigh, at a time when that organisation completed the largest sports diving programme ever mounted anywhere in the world.

This fascinating book details more than 10 years of exciting diving, beginning with those early days in Ulster; taking the reader through adventurous exploits in the warm seas of Italy, Gibraltar and Cyprus; and culminating in such exotic underwater haunts as Hong Kong, Fiji and the Caribbean.

Ned vividly describes the pleasures derived from hours spent underwater with Killer Whales and dolphins; the dizzy effects of nitrogen narcosis poisoning at a depth of 70 metres (230 feet); the excitement of exploring the Blue Hole off Belize, first highlighted by Jacques Cousteau; as well as the humorous antics of his diving partners along the way. He recounts a tragic attempt to rescue two Chinese illegal immigrants in Hong Kong and explains what to do when confronted with an unexploded World War Two mine!

Ned, throughout his adventurous narrative, stresses the extreme importance of sound basic training in underwater skills.

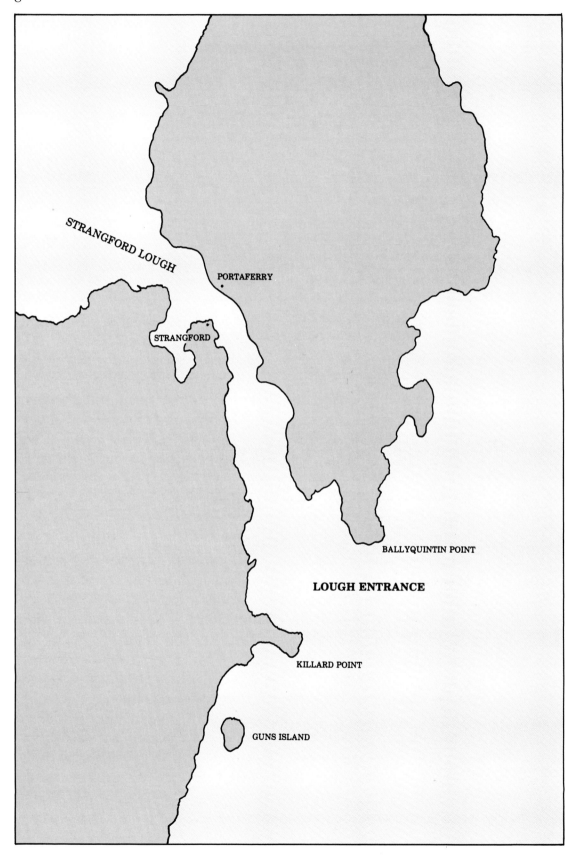

STRANGFORD LOUGH

PORTAFERRY

STRANGFORD

BALLYQUINTIN POINT

LOUGH ENTRANCE

KILLARD POINT

GUNS ISLAND

CHAPTER ONE
Where It All Began
1975

LIKE so many others, my initiation into scuba diving came through an enjoyment of spear-fishing. Working in Northern Ireland and living on the shores of Dundrum Bay, I was shown how to use mask, snorkel and fins and was so impressed that, on the following weekend, I arrived back on the beach with my own equipment. Up to that point I had always feared the unknown lurking under the water's surface—even the slimy touch of some unseen weed could be very disconcerting, especially since I was not a strong swimmer. Now, suddenly, all these worries had disappeared; with the aid of my facemask I could penetrate the mysterious depths and would often part the weed and swim right through.

This new world of underwater creatures was as exciting as the fields and hedgerows I had discovered as a child: we caught lobster and crab and, occasionally, speared a decent fish for supper. It was a glorious summer, one which we did not wish to see end. By October we had donned wetsuits, black suits of foam neoprene rubber that enabled us to stay in the water long after the swimmers had given up visiting the beaches. One sunny afternoon, having swum out to a pair of rocks called the 'Cow and Calf' about one mile offshore, I was basking in the sun, well satisfied with my lobster catch and contemplating the return journey, when I realised just how much my swimming had improved over the past months. I had always wanted to learn how to dive but thought that my swimming ability would let me down. Perhaps it was time to find out.....

I started by joining a diving club at Lisburn run by Marc Moody; the diving officer was our good friend the late Mal Newman. During those cold winter months of 1975, I soaked up all the training the club, a branch of the British Sub-Aqua Club (BSAC), could throw at me. I was deeply impressed with their thoroughness and attention to detail; undoubtedly this good grounding in the sport would serve me well in the years to come.

● *Opposite*: The entrance to Strangford Lough, Northern Ireland. Ecologically, this lough is one of the most interesting underwater environments in Europe.

South of Belfast lies Strangford Lough, ecologically one of the most interesting underwater environments in Europe. The lough is connected to the coast by a narrow stretch of water some five miles long. This narrow passage runs between the towns of Strangford, in County Down, and Portaferry, on the 'Ards peninsula, and is the setting for some of the most violent currents I have ever seen as the waters within the lough rise and fall with successive tides. Many years ago, Jacques Cousteau on his famous research vessel the Calypso came to study and film the marine life shaped by the special features of this unique lough. Killer Whales have been sighted here on more than one occasion, and I have seen a large school of dolphins. It was at Ballywhite Bay, just north of Portaferry, that I undertook my first dive. We entered the water with Mal Newman, the dive leader, at 2.30 pm precisely. Our entry was made a little more difficult by a slightly choppy sea; however, we were soon underneath the mild turbulence and I was taking the first faltering steps on an exciting adventure that, little did I realise, was to take me right across the world.

We drifted along at a steady pace while Marc followed our progress from the surface in an inflatable boat. All manner of living creatures swam and ran before us; we lifted large fronds of kelp and watched while the exposed crabs scurried away. I could hardly contain my excitement. I clearly recall coming across a large high-pressure air cylinder and being abruptly stopped from any close examination. Mal later explained that, if the cylinder was still charged, it could possibly explode. It was not long after this that Mal gave the signal to surface and we were picked up by the boat. I can relive almost every moment of that first dive.

Marc and I have become firm friends over the years, although our association at the time lasted for only six months or so. In that short period I had learned a lot, not only about scuba diving but also about life in a diving club.

In the June of 1976 I was transferred to Germany but, before leaving Ulster, I saw something underwater which has remained etched in my mind and is as clear today as it was on that first memorable sighting. My fellow club members had gone to the south of France for their annual expedition and, being unable to participate because of my impending move, I teamed up with some local divers for a trip to the Maiden Islands.

The Maidens, once known as the Nine Maids, are situated due east of Larne. The largest two islands support lighthouses although only one of these is currently in use: both were fully operative before World War Two, but the glass domes were dismantled at the outbreak of hostilities. Many a German submarine mistook the dark, twin lighthouses for the twin stacks of a capital ship of the Royal Navy only to expend a valuable torpedo on barren rock.

We set off from the small port of Glenarm, north of Larne, finally dropping anchor next to Allen Rock, only just visible at low tide; the journey having taken almost two hours in a ship's lifeboat that barely managed a speed of five knots. One of a team of four, I dived deeper that day than ever before; 80, 90, 100 feet before I was finally standing on the seabed. At that point I was probably more interested in 'doing the ton' than anything else but I was impressed with the clarity of the water at that depth—an obvious advantage to being so far from the shore.

Our leader, having indicated that we should follow, set off past all sorts of wreckage; a mast which we swam under as it rested against a large rock, some rigging, and what looked like a large funnel. We eventually circumnavigated the base of the rock next to which we were anchored; on our left, large kelp fronds covering a steep slope pointed towards the surface like a million outstretched fingers and, to our right, stretched an expanse of dark deep water. We finally rounded the last bend and there she was....

This was something totally unexpected. Up until now I had assumed that a few well-flattened metal plates in fairly shallow water qualified for the 'wreck dive' entry in my logbook—but not now. This ship right in front of me was truly magnificent. Looking as she must have done on launching day, the intact ship sat upright on the seabed, her decks with a swept clean appearance and her bow disappearing into the rocky slope. The latter undoubtedly kept her upright and the kelp fronds hid the damage she sustained when she first ran aground. It was as though some giant hand had placed this vessel with great care for the sole purpose of impressing the occasional visitor such as myself!

This ship had plied its trade across the seven seas only to founder a few miles from port. I could see the deep keel as it rested on the seabed, the curve of the stern with its enormous propeller still in place. It took only the slightest imagination to visualise the crew at their stations—loading, unloading, or sailing across a calm sea. All too soon the dive was over and there were a million things I had not done. All my time had been spent getting to the wreck and attempting to take in the incredible sight—perhaps there would be another chance for a closer examination.

The wreck—the Spanish tramp steamer 'Albia of Santander'

On the 28th of September 1929 the 'Albia', loaded with ore and bound for Belfast, ran aground on Allen rock. The Donaghadee lifeboat and the tug Audacious from Belfast successfully landed the entire crew. The 'Albia' remained aground for several months, during which time most of her cargo was salvaged, before slipping quietly beneath the waves at the onset of an early summer storm in 1930. She has remained almost undisturbed ever since.

Less than two weeks later I left Ulster for Germany. Since that day, over 10 years ago, I have been most fortunate in being able to dive all over the world. From as far north as Norway to as far south as Fiji, I have seen many breathtaking sights beneath the waves, but none to equal that vision on Allen Rock.

● Taff Jones on the wheelhouse of the 'Lochgarry'.

CHAPTER TWO
On The Continent
1976-1977

I moved to Wildenrath, a small West German town close to the Dutch border and, although miles from the sea, there was still plenty of opportunity for diving, especially since Alan Forster ran a very good branch of the BSAC nearby. Alan, a man of many talents, not only a diving instructor but also National Instructor and First Class Diver, is a former sergeant in the French Foreign Legion and speaks several European languages fluently. Having completed about 30 dives before leaving Ulster, my diving was still in its infancy, however, once I had been taken under Alan's wing, my training progressed rapidly and, within a year, I too qualified as an instructor.

The diving in Germany was largely confined to freshwater lakes, quarries and reservoirs, some of which were far better than others. The dives themselves were almost invariably confined to training as the opportunity for a serious dive with an objective was rather limited. We did strive to add variety wherever possible and names such as Beuel Quarry, Fussenich Lake, Venekotensee, Woffelsbach Reservoir and Schiefbahn Lake appeared in my logbook on successive weekends.

In early 1977 I was introduced to the dubious delights of ice-diving. Having driven to Venekotensee on a very cold but clear January morning, I was partnered for the proposed dive with Chris Andrews, our new diving officer. His planning was meticulous, as it had to be on any dive, but ice-diving, like cave-diving, does not allow the diver to simply surface should something go wrong. He drove a large metal stake firmly into the bank, and then fixed one end of a long rope, appropriately called a lifeline, to the stake and tied the other end to himself.

Attached to each other by means of a buddy line, we entered the water through a hole in the ice, remaining close together throughout the 10 metres (33 feet) dive. We spotted the occasional fish in a state of semi-hibernation, but there was little really to recommend the dive. The one lesson I vividly remember was my total inability to cut through the thin ice with my knife. Above the seabed and treading water, I tried very hard to penetrate the ice but only succeeded in pushing myself away from the solid surface. Had my feet been on the lake bed, I would have had no trouble in pushing a hole through. This really only served to emphasise the need for sound planning when undertaking such a dive. We followed our lifeline back to the hole and left the water. I remember it was bitterly cold and the passing Germans, out for a stroll near the lake, must have thought us quite mad. There doesn't really seem to be a lot of excitement in diving under freshwater ice; the salty environment of warmer climes, abounding with marine life, is so much more interesting. I cannot believe that this kind of ice-diving will prove as popular as wreck or cave-diving; however, the complete instructor is one who has undertaken most, if not all, aspects of the sport and consequently instructs from the vantage point of personal experience.

If there was one great advantage to being in Germany it was the opportunity for mounting expeditions. My stay there lasted 18 months and, during this time, I visited Monte Christo off the west coast of Italy, Norway, Elba and Gibraltar.

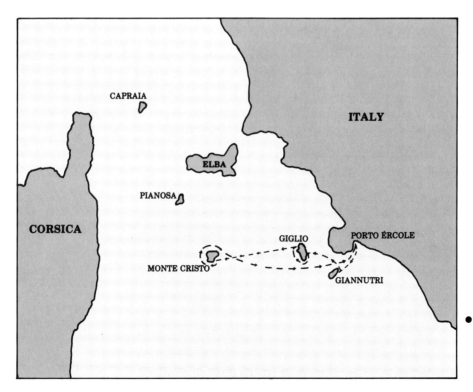

● The west coast of Italy showing the route taken by 'Fieramosca' during April 1977.

Expedition Deepstar '77.

Expedition members:	Alan Forster—Leader.
	Chris Andrews—Diving Officer.
	Vic Shepheard, Len Lees,
	Philip Cross, Peter Weilgosch,
	Hugh Manuel, Self.
Vessel:	'Fieramosca', 46ft, converted
	wooden trawler launched 1936.
Skipper:	Rudy and his lovely lady Ilsa.
Home Port:	Porto Ercole, west coast of
	Italy.

On 10th April 1977 we sailed from Porto Ercole to commence a most interesting trip, and one which gave me a valuable insight into life onboard a small ship as well as deep-diving. However, I did not get off to a good start—the trip to Giannutri took less than two hours and I was the first to be seasick! Having missed the first dive as a result of my illness, I aborted a later dive after only four or five minutes in the water. A storm blew up on that first night and a shifting wind found us in an exposed bay. We all took turns to man the bilge pump and it was some time before we had the water down to a level where the ship's pumps could take control. Needless to say, I was rapidly becoming disillusioned with the trip, but things quickly improved. After a good nights sleep, we all felt much better and were ready for the day's diving activities. My first dive in the Mediterranean, amongst its colourful and prolific fish, lasted for almost 40 minutes and was a complete success.

We were nearing the end of that first dive and heading back towards the boat when we came across Chris and Peter swimming in the same direction. Chris had a passion for octopus and had already caught one when we came across another pair. Chris played with one for a short time, insisting that they became tired very quickly, and then placed the exhausted creature under his armpit where it hung on very tightly. He was happily tackling his third octopus when the first one, having recovered somewhat, climbed around his side, up over his aqualung and onto the back of his head. Chris himself felt none of this activity as he was clad in a thick wetsuit but, at this point, the octopus reached over and pulled the facemask from his face! I hasten to add that the removal and replacement of diving equipment underwater is well practised and the incident presented no harm to our illustrious diving officer, except to his pride as he ended up losing all three of his captives.

The object of the expedition was, quite simply, deep diving. My logbook reads 26, 35, 39, 40, 45 and 50 metres (165 feet) for the first six dives of the trip. The idea was to get down to the required depth and remain at that depth for the planned bottom time, thus preparing ourselves thoroughly for the deeper dives to come.

There were two important considerations for every dive. The first was decompression sickness and the second nitrogen narcosis poisoning (known as the 'narcs'). We did not have a recompression chamber onboard and there were none to be found this far from the Italian mainland. Therefore, each dive had to be carefully planned in terms of depth, time and ascent, in order to avoid 'the bends' through sound planning as opposed to trusting to luck. We carried a complete set of decompression tables supplied by the Royal Naval Physiological Laboratory and these covered depths up to 75 metres. The 'narcs', however, affects each individual in a different way and consequently there are no charts to tell the dive leader at what depth a diver may become affected.

When a diver descends slowly he eventually reaches a depth, not normally before 30 metres (100 feet), where he becomes aware of a light-headed feeling similar to that associated with being tipsy after a few drinks: to ascend a few feet removes the feeling altogether, whereas to descend still further reinforces the sensation and leads to the impairment of sound judgment. At this point, a diver may go deeper than intended and consequently black-out, or he may remain much longer than originally planned, running the risk of decompression sickness or even running out of air. Allowing the dives to become progressively deeper enables the diver to build up an immunity to the effects of the 'narcs': although everyone in our team was affected to some degree at 70 metres, the effects were certainly minimised.

Cala Ischiaiola, a bay on the island of Giannutri, harbours an interesting wreck at 40 metres. Having swum down the anchor line we could clearly see, from as shallow as 10 metres, the wrecked vessel, fairly intact and lying on its side, the bronze propeller still in place. The ship had apparently sunk during a bad storm as recently as 1971. Early the next morning we vis-

ited the wreck once again and, although I was carrying sufficient air for the planned dive, I used so much in a vain attempt
to remove a brass lamp that I had to breathe from a spare
cylinder during my decompression stop. Lesson learned!

On the 13th we departed for Giglio to resupply before sailing for Monte Christo. There was time for a full breakfast and
a few souvenirs before returning to the ship; I well remember
the top priority on the shopping list being fresh bread!

Monte Christo is comprised of a single block of granite in
the middle of nowhere, sheer cliffs rising out of the water
promising some very good diving. We were not disappointed.
We commenced our diving at Cala Del Diavolo where I first saw
moray eel and crayfish. I constantly practised the need to dou-
ble check the dive plan against my watch and depth gauge
while under the influence of the 'narcs'. This was achieved
satisfactorily, but normal mental activity became a laboured
conscious effort of single consecutive thoughts.

Throughout the following days, our diving remained at 45
to 50 metres as we prepared ourselves for the deeper diving to
come. However, each plunge was a first-class excursion into a
superb marine environment; constantly surrounded by millions
of fish, we even hand-fed them as we whiled away our decompression times.

Being partial to lobster I, along with everyone else onboard, was keen to try crayfish. Chris said he would take us to
a reef, not far away, where we would find one in every hole. We
found the reef easily and it was clear from Chris's hand signals
that he wanted us to watch him in order to learn how it was
done. After a few attempts he finally had hold of one—well almost. As the crayfish struggled, Chris tried to keep a tight hold
but only succeeded in dropping it again before finally getting a
good grip and stuffing the creature into his dive-bag. Certainly
it was a good size and he proudly displayed his trophy with an
unmistakable 'that's the way to do it' expression on his face.
Peter and I promptly held up our bags bulging with a pair of
crayfish in each. At this juncture Chris once again demon-
strated his expert knowledge of hand signals!

We had one more wreck dive, known as the 'Cup Wreck',
on the agenda. Although a vast area of seabed is strewn with
wreckage, there is little that can be identified as a specific part
of a ship. Her cargo of white cups and white tiles litter the
seabed by the thousands. Alan told us of a previous trip when

● Some of the diving
in Italy was quite
spectacular. At one
point, we were 230
feet down off the
coast of Monte
Cristo.

he and Chris found a hole occupied by a very large lobster. Unfortunately, the lobster was lodged very far into the hole and had defied all attempts to remove it. Chris led my group, which was first in the water, and Alan led the second group. We had been on the wreck for a short while when Chris found the hole and beckoned to us. Each of my three partners having gazed into the empty hole before my turn came, I was just about to turn away when a slight movement caught my eye–the biggest conger eel I have ever seen came forward to the entrance and returned my startled stare.

I couldn't help but grin at the thought of Alan finding the hole and looking right in, expecting to get another chance at a very big lobster.

We were approaching the end of the trip and the time was right for the deepest dives. The location was Punta Della Piana, which we reached in our inflatable boat. Alan took the lead as soon as we entered the water and we stayed together, although the trip down was very fast. Finally Alan stopped and stood on a rock at 70 metres surrounded by the torchlit Red Coral we had come all this way to see. Red Coral is much sought after and expensive to buy carved into intricate figures, just as ivory is carved in the Far East. However, our motives were not so mercenary and we were quite happy to chip away and collect a small fragment as a souvenir.

Ten minutes after we entered the water we had to leave the bottom to commence the return journey. Less than eight minutes were actually spent at 70 metres and this meant a decompression schedule of 30 minutes on the way back. We returned to 70 metres again, later the same day, and that left only one more dive before sailing back to Porto Ercole.

The overall trip had been a tremendous success and remains a great credit to both Alan and Chris, who jointly shared the overall responsibility. The experience of diving to 70 metres was well worth the effort and the cost, although I doubt whether such diving on a regular basis is a viable proposition from the amateur viewpoint.

In May 1977 I moved to Soest and formed a diving club, taking on the mantle of diving officer for the first time. Three English school teachers joined the club and I got on very well with two of them, but they eventually stopped attending as the diving in West German lakes was not quite what they expected.

The third member of that illustrious trio, a young swimming teacher and former competition swimmer called Jenny, was very strong in the water so that the training presented very few problems for her; however, we just did not get on. I think about six months had passed before we finally became good friends and, the following year, we were married in Chester.

In August 1977 I spent five weeks in Norway on an expedition run by my good friend Mike Law. Twelve members of the Dortmund Sub-Aqua Club were joined by a similar number of students from Durham University. It was nice to be back in the sea again on a regular basis, but the work was conducted in such a way that it was only of interest to the young scientists. Counting specimens and observing behaviour can be made interesting to the layman; however, the divers from Dortmund were largely required to complete the more boring tasks and generally nursemaid the students.

I returned to Soest on 5th September and was immediately invited to lead an expedition to Gibraltar for two weeks in November. Would I like to go? Marc Moody was in Gibraltar at that time and I was looking forward to seeing him once again. The details of this trip and another in 1981 are covered in Chapter Seven.

CHAPTER THREE
A Dive On High Explosives
1978

1978 was a year of complete contrast. In February I moved to Chester and, although Jenny and I honeymooned in Elba where we did manage a few dives (including Jenny's first trip to 100 feet), work became my only priority as I was being considered for promotion.

We regularly visited the North Wales coast at weekends and it was here that I met Alan Barnes, a businessman from Leicester. Alan kept a powerful Dory at Pwllheli and we regularly dived the coast of Bardsey Island looking for crayfish.

On the 27th August we stopped for lunch on the south of the island just below the lighthouse. Alan and I then decided to enter the water right where we were in order to see what this small bay had to offer. With the Dory above us in the safe hands of Graham Platt, Alan and I descended to 16 metres. The seabed was very uneven, consisting of mud and rocky outcrops, and after some 15 minutes we turned and headed back. Alan was well over to my right, the distance between us increasing a little as I skirted a large rock. Immediately behind that rock was what can only be described as a large egg sitting on the seabed. It was in fact a mine ..... to be more precise, an admiralty pattern, Mk 17, World War Two mine.

● Exploring the rocks off the west coast of Bardsey Island.

● *Opposite*: Jenny

At this point Alan had not seen it and my immediate reaction was to simply put as many miles between myself and IT as rapidly as possible. However, those initial thoughts quickly gave way to reason. We were very friendly with the Bardsey fishermen and their pots were placed all over this bay; it was possible that, at any time, one of those pots could land on top of this device with disastrous consequences. The other consideration was that, since the mine was at least 40 years old, assuming it remained untouched, there was no reason why it should suddenly explode.

Numerous authorities, such as the police, coastguard and naval bomb disposal experts, would need to know about the device and they were sure to ask a lot of questions. Unfortunately, I was unprepared for taking notes and had no means of measuring the mine. I tried to visualise the questions that would be asked. Where? What size? Description? Depth? Then there would be that one final question which would make reporting the mine pointless unless I answered 'yes'—'can you find it again?'

I began by judging its width and length against my own dimensions. Glancing quickly at Alan, I could see that he was heading towards me: this was fortunate as I had made mental notes of certain features and wanted to surface immediately above the device in order to establish its position in relation to the shore. We lifted off from the seabed and I positioned myself above the mine as we rose to the surface. As soon as I broke surface, I took a bearing on a prominent rock and asked Graham to estimate our distance from the shore. I then tried to write it all down as quickly as I could.

We returned to Pwllheli and reported the matter to the local police who, in turn, informed the coastguard and the naval bomb and mine disposal unit. I told the navy that I was reasonably certain of being able to find the mine again so they travelled up from Plymouth, arriving on the evening of the following day.

The bomb disposal team was comprised of three men led by Chief Petty Officer Les Wood, a remarkable man with countless stories that never ceased to amuse us.

The following morning we set off from Pwllheli, picking up Les and his team at Aberdaron on the way. I remember Alan handing me the keys to his Dory, he said it was my show and I might just need a boat. Anchoring in the general area, Alan and I kitted up for the first dive of the day. Our task was to find the mine, examine it in the light of instructions given by Les and leave a marker buoy close by–all without touching it. Descending down the anchor line, we commenced our search and had not gone far when Alan, swimming off to his left, signalled back to me. He had found the mine not 20 metres from the anchor. We secured the buoy and, after a visual inspection of the device, surfaced and left the rest to the professionals.

Using a charge of eight pounds of plastic explosives, the device was detonated at precisely 3 pm. To the disappointment of all the sightseers who had gathered in a flotilla of small boats, only the charge exploded, not the mine itself. However, a follow-up dive two days later revealed that the mine had certainly disintegrated and we recovered a large piece of the casing which now hangs in Pwllheli Power Boat Club.

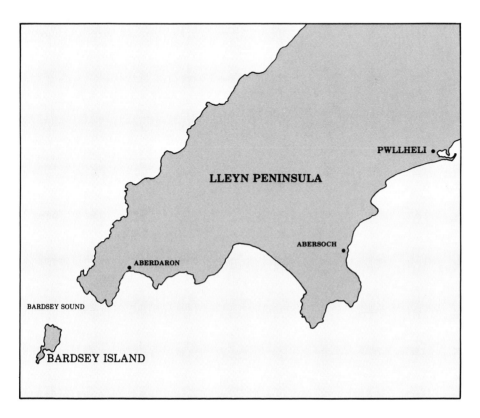

● Bardsey Island, North Wales.

● A colourful Hong
Kong market scene.

CHAPTER FOUR
Hong Kong
1979-1981

JENNY and I had two memorable years with the Gurkhas in Hong Kong. Coincidentally, that tour commenced with the birth of our eldest daughter Beth, in April 1979, and ended with the birth of our son Daniel, in April 1981. So, for a number of reasons, we look back on those years with a great deal of affection.

It was also during those very years that Hong Kong commanded much of the attention of the world's press. The illegal immigrants from communist China continued to stretch the security forces, while, at the same time, the Vietnamese refugee problem was far from solved.

Geographically, Hong Kong is comprised of Hong Kong island, Lantau island, the Kowloon peninsula, that area of countryside north of Kowloon called the New Territories (which is ceded to Britain by a lease agreement due to expire in 1997) and a number of small islands mainly to the south and east; altogether some 407 square miles.

At first sight, one feels that the opportunities for some really first class diving must be endless; some of the smaller islands certainly look like attractive dive sites. Oddly enough, they even bear a striking resemblance to parts of Norway and

● Hong Kong Boat People.

North Wales where the diving is rather good. In addition, the region qualifies as a sub-tropical zone, where the sea temperatures ranged from 10°C. to 33°C. during my first year there. The terrain is such that large hills dominate the scenery and roll sharply down to the South China Sea.

However, just one dive will dispel all hopes of really superb diving. It just does not exist and the reasons for this have never ceased to fascinate me. To begin with, there are three prime ingredients for good sports diving; good underwater visibility, a certain amount of depth and an interesting location. Remove any one of these and you should still have a good dive, remove any two, or even three and, to be honest, you have Hong Kong.

A number of factors contribute to the extremely poor underwater visibility prevalent in the area. In the first place, the hills are geologically very ancient and are simply crumbling. The problem of landslips, especially after heavy rain, is a fact of life in the colony. Reclamation is also taking place in which massive areas of hillside are literally being transported and dumped into the sea by an endless supply of trucks. As a result, great clouds of fine sandy soil are washed into the sea by successive rainfalls, taking ages to disperse and finally settle. Extensive pollution also takes its toll on visibility levels and has even more far reaching consequences for the environment as a whole. Hong Kong harbour, one of the busiest in the world, seems to play host to almost every kind of pollutant devised by man; raw human sewage alongside untreated industrial waste flow freely into the sea.

I have watched the rivers and streams in the New Territories change colour as well as consistency, the aromas from these open sewers being seldom pleasant. Pass by any laundry and you will see great quantities of soapy water running straight into the local stream–it too, eventually finds its way into the sea.

The absence of any real depth is a disadvantage in itself, but it is also a major contributor to the lack of good visibility. Immediately to the west of Hong Kong, on the Chinese mainland, lies the Pearl River estuary which, over the centuries, has poured tons of silt into the South China Sea. This silt has settled in large quantities around the colony to the extent that the waters are disappointingly shallow. Despite these drawbacks, there is still a thriving diving community, but most of the divers spend their time in depths of less than 15 metres, often less than 10 metres.

Curiously, the scenery above the surface belies the true situation found beneath the waves; those steep green slopes that roll sharply down to the waters edge stop almost as soon as they dip beneath the surface.

Finally we come to the third element under the guise of 'interesting underwater location'–the marine environment itself. Before we proceed it would help to understand some of the attitudes of the Chinese people towards the sea. Through centuries of necessity, the Chinese have learned the importance of using every means available to them in the production of food for hungry mouths. What is not consumed is turned into a profit of one form or another.

It is all too easy to simply criticise but such criticism can be unfair since, in the final analysis, absolutely nothing is wasted. However, it is a sad fact that there are no laws in relation to the minimum sizes of fish which may be removed from the sea. Similarly, since there is no legislation to control mesh sizes for fishing nets, those used are very fine and consequently very effective even for the smallest of fish.

The prime edible fish go straight to market. Fishing vessels are met at the quayside by small lorries carrying large tanks of salt water and the fish are loaded, transported and generally sold live; some will remain alive longer than others in large aquaria as they grace the entrances to restaurants until selected by customers for their evening meal.

The larger junks do not always put to sea and are often seen working in pairs, dredging the seabed very close to the shore. To dive in the ecological disaster area left behind by one of these operations is to enter a barren seascape: no fish, no coral, no marine creatures at all, only a set of skid marks across the seabed to bear temporary witness to their passing.

The much smaller sampans drop lines of wire-mesh caskets further inshore in a bid to catch the smaller reef fishes, crabs and even hermit crabs. Some of these caskets are no larger than a cubic foot with an extremely fine mesh, others may be bigger; but, in any event, there is no doubt that it is the smaller fish that are sought.

The effect of this silt-laden water, pollution and over-fishing is an underwater drabness that stands in stark contrast to those pictures of bright lights and high-rise buildings which are synonymous with Hong Kong. It is possibly the only tropical water in the entire world where a diver can find an expanse of coral and actually have to search before finding a single tropical fish.

Of course the sea is a great diluter and, even in these waters, one will find areas of interest. To my untrained eye it seemed that the scavengers thrived particularly well. Quite often these are the most accessible and interesting of marine creatures. Sea slugs (*Nudibranchia*) were to be found in great variety—at one time almost every dive seemed to turn up a new specimen. Long-spined sea-urchins (*Diadema*) also occurred in their thousands—too many for my liking! Any contact with the long spines usually results in several pieces embedded under the skin. Unfortunately, once these spines have broken off they lose their brittleness and turn septic. While experienced divers have no trouble in avoiding them, the novice often discovers these creatures by dropping feet first onto them at the beginning of a dive.

Apart from a variety of crabs, hermit crabs, cowries and other types of shell-fish, there are an encouraging number of anemones, especially *Tealia coriaces*, which supply numerous refuges for the very colourful Clark's Anemonefish, *Amphiprion clarkii*. Damselfish, particularly the Yellow-Tailed Damselfish (*Pomacentrus melanchir*), Scorpionfish and White-Spotted Blowfish (*Arothron hispidus*) are encountered on most dives.

● A junk at anchor in the New Territories.

Certainly all is not lost, but the underwater scene is dismal and the problems daunting. During my stay, I was the diving officer of the New Territories Diving Club as well as a member of the Hong Kong Underwater Club. My role as diving officer was largely confined to training, whereas my outings with the Underwater Club were for the pure enjoyment of diving. They

● *Above: Conus textile.* Textile cone shells were particularly prolific in Hong Kong. A worldwide survey of known stings from textile cones revealed that twenty seven out of thirty recorded cases proved fatal.

● A long-spined sea-urchin (*Centrostephanus longispinus*).

complimented each other perfectly and I have many happy memories of my association with both clubs.

In April 1980 I attended a number of examinations over a two week period and qualified as an Advanced Instructor and First Class Diver. By this time I had logged over 300 dives and had amassed experiences from a number of different countries.

The most memorable experience during my stay was a series of four dives spread over a fortnight. The dives included meeting, touching and photographing sharks, dolphins and even a Killer Whale underwater. However, even though the water was up to 23 feet deep, I was not in the sea. The story began when I first visited Ocean Park with my family. This leisure facility boasts the largest saltwater aquarium in the world, an arena where dolphins and a Killer Whale called Hoi Wai perform, a Wave Cove where seals, penguins and pelicans can be seen in a natural setting and lots more besides.

Many a diver's first reaction on seeing the aquarium is an overwhelming desire to dive in, and mine was no different. The aquarium, 'Atoll Reef', holds 400,000 gallons of water and is so carefully designed that the inhabitants can be viewed from above the surface and from below at various levels. Each time the visitor goes down to the next level, the glass is that much thicker and a little darker.

The visitor is treated to a 'diver's eye view' of a tropical reef complete with a variety of fish that would be hard to find, all in one place, anywhere in the world. In the centre of the aquarium, a tall pillar of rock rises from the seabed and forms an island (the atoll) at the surface. A variety of fish, including a large shoal of batfish (*Platax pinnatus*) and another of Blue-Lined Snapper (*Lutjanus kasmira*), swim through the water-column whilst the smaller angel and butterfly fish, as beautiful as their names suggest, dabble closer to the surface. In the middle levels we spotted sharks, with attached Remoras, lazily circling. Among the carefully arranged coral outcrops, moray eels, grouper and the occasional puffer fish could be seen— there was also a splendid pair of Bull-Nosed Wrasse. At the lowest level, the floor of the aquarium was littered with resting sharks lying side by side. The darkening glass added to the overall effect by giving an impression of far greater depth.

Shortly after this visit, I heard that they required a diver to take photographs inside the aquarium. Needless to say I applied for the job, but it was not that simple and I was turned down. About a year later, having improved considerably as a photographer, I inquired once again and, on this occasion, I picked the right time.

I was met by a very charming girl called Judy Wu–the Park's chief diver. Every piece of diving equipment had to be thoroughly washed before being allowed near the water. The entrance to the aquarium was cleverly concealed behind a mock-up scene of a South Pacific shoreline and my final instructions were that I should not damage the corals, especially those directly beneath me, as I entered.

I was required to produce a number of photographs of the inhabitants and then do the same thing in the main arena. I disturbed the larger sharks as I entered the water and they proceeded to swim around at various depths. Using a 20mm wide angle lens, I had no problem framing the whole shark; however, I changed to the 28mm lens for the smaller fish. The only inhabitant to bother me was a Nurse Shark, but I followed instructions and struck it on the nose with my knuckles two or three times until it got the message.

As soon as I emerged, it was time to meet Hoi Wai, the Killer Whale. If ever there was a misnomer, this was it–Hoi Wai was as gentle as a Giant Panda. By way of introduction I sat on the side of the pool and began to stroke her chin, whereupon she lifted her fin out of the water to show me just where she wanted to be tickled–some killer! Even so, I still entered the water carefully for I had no intention of frightening this beautiful creature, especially as I was unsure of her reaction to a pair of powerful strobes. At first she was a little difficult both in her holding pen and in the main arena: one particular dolphin had become her special companion and she became upset when they were not together. The solution was simple and, as soon as the dolphins joined us, Hoi Wai's character completely changed.

The dolphins' reaction to the flash units was interesting: a group would approach to within a metre or two and stop, applying some powerful but invisible braking system, and as I took a photograph they would dash off to the far corner of the pool only to regroup and approach once again. Occasionally, they wouldn't stop but continued right past. Curiously, as Hoi Wai's tail was just about to brush against me as she passed by, she would lift it, avoiding me completely.

Once the Park's authorities had seen the photographs,

● Hoi Wai, a young female Killer Whale (*Orca orcinus*). The dorsal fin on a male adult Killer Whale can grow to over six feet.

they raised more questions than I had anticipated and so I was invited to go through the whole process again, looking for some specific shots. This time I took along a diving buddy of mine from the New Territories Club, 'Dick' Turpin. He changed film for me while I was inside the Atoll Reef, but I asked him to join me in the arena when I went to visit the whale and dolphins.

Dick was carrying an underwater movie camera and I thought nothing of this until it was turned on; the almost imperceptible noise from the drive-unit was clearly heard by all the mammals and had them completely baffled. At times they became so inquisitive that it was difficult to separate them from Dick in order to take photographs. They became more and more playful, coming closer and closer; often it seemed the dolphins were looking straight at me through the camera. At one time, I was so completely surrounded by dolphins that the only way for Hoi Wai to get in the act was to swim right through my legs.

Each of the four dives had lasted two hours, a total of eight of the most satisfying hours I had ever spent underwater. The end result was over 200 photographs and quite a story to tell my friends. The curator of Atoll Reef, Johnny Chin, travels all over the world looking for specimens for his aquarium and invited me to join him on a trip into China to take even more underwater photographs. Now there was a chance to make a little bit of history—unfortunately the trip was planned for 1981 when I would be back in England......

When things go wrong

Ping Chau, the remotest of all the islands surrounding Hong Kong, has a small military presence, continually renewed and resupplied by Wessex helicopters from the New Territories. If there was sufficient room and a return flight later in the day, we might be offered a lift by one of the pilots. That is how I, and six of my colleagues, came to be flying over Ping Chau early one morning in February 1981.

As dive leader I was given a set of headphones and a throat microphone, so that I was privy to the conversations within the aircraft. At one time I heard the co-pilot mention something about fuel and the pilot replied that it was low but not critical. We had selected Grass Island for the diving and, as we approached, the pilot said he would circle the island so that I could pick the best spot. As we came around the exposed side I saw in the distance, for a brief moment, two black blobs in the water. The pilot had also spotted the objects and, within a short time, we were directly over them.

Each blob turned out to be a lorry inner tube, each carrying two illegal immigrants from China. One vessel had developed a leak and the occupants were in serious trouble. For obvious reasons, illegal immigrants make the best use of the hours of darkness in their bid to escape to Hong Kong, therefore, it is likely that this pair had set off from China, shortly after sunset on the previous day: at the very least, they would have been in the water for twelve hours, possibly sixteen. By the time we saw them, the two craft were about a mile apart; the sea rough, with an opposing strong wind. Their only means of propulsion being crude wooden paddles, there was no way that they could even assist each other.

The pilot decided to drop the diving party immediately, but I stayed onboard to assist. I quickly changed into my wetsuit. Unfortunately, the helicopter was not fitted with a winch: it did, however, carry a thick green hawser attached above the open door and with a metal fitting at one end. Keeping the other end of the hawser inside the aircraft, the crewman fed out a large loop, the pilot hovering as close to the waves as possible; this manoeuvre required a high degree of skill, courage and determination. The intention was that the crewman and I would then try and pull each man into the aircraft. The downdraft created by the helicopter proved a major obstacle; not only was this extremely powerful but, in February, bitterly cold also. By this time the two men were floundering in the sea desperately struggling to swim and, although the downdraft flattened an area around the victims it also created a violent, ice cold spindrift.

The men were already well on their way to becoming exposure victims and were not in a position to help themselves, a situation exacerbated by their exhausted state. There was no alternative, I quickly entered the water beside them. Pulling them back to their raft which was still able to give a minimal amount of buoyancy and finally attaching the end of the green hawser to the craft, I prepared for a long tow to shore. As any lifesaving instructor will confirm, when one comes across a real victim, even during the initial struggle, a few words of reassurance will help to instil calm. The rescuer then explains to the victim the need to relax and just concentrate on breathing. Now try and explain that to two Chinese who understood neither the language nor the gestures, possibly not even the reassuring calm tones of my voice: what they did appreciate was the seriousness of the situation, clinging to me for dear life, wrapping their arms and legs around me. Each time this happened, I had to submerge, push them away, surface and start again. In the end, pulling them by the hair seemed to be the most effective way of getting back to the frail craft. Several times the journey to the nearest island was interrupted as a result of panic and, all this time, the fuel situation was getting even lower. Undoubtedly it was the longest journey of my life; pounded by the sea's icy spray as we were pulled along, I was physically holding two men but gradually losing my grip on one of them. Finally, I could hold him no longer and, leaving the remaining victim with the craft, I swam after him. The pilot, noticing what had happened, dragged the craft round in a slow circle to meet me. In the meantime, I caught the missing man and went through all the struggles and panic again until the craft reached us. We set off yet again.

This time I lost the other hapless Chinese and the process of rescue with all its attendant problems began once more. The aircraft flew sideways, low over the waves, the most incredible piece of flying I have ever witnessed–only one of those waves had to hit the helicopter to bring it down. I desperately wanted to tell the pilot to slow down, but he could do no more. However, the wash finally had all three of us in the water together. While the craft was slowly brought around, one last time, I held on to both the unfortunate men, aided by nothing more than the buoyancy in my suit. This time, I wedged myself into the deflated inner tube with one of the Chinese in each of my arms, they were very, very frightened and totally unable to help themselves.

The journey seemed endless, the spray biting, but this time we held on and the rocks of the island of Kung Chau were getting closer. On seeing dry land, one of the Chinese who had held onto a small, inflatable pillow throughout the ordeal, left us and made a swim for the island. It was obvious that we should concentrate on the remaining victim. Since there was no place for the helicopter to land, our pilot towed us as close

● *Above*: Dolphins at Ocean Park.

● *Right*: Clark's Anemonefish (*Amphiprion clarkii*), commonly known as a clownfish. These little fish live in and around anemones poisonous to all other fish.

● *Far right*: A Leopard Shark from Atoll Reef. Note the Remora or Suckerfish attached to the shark's body.

as possible; flying over the rocks, he drew us right by them. Clinging onto the stony terrain with one hand and the victim with the other, I tried to push him up but he wanted no part of it—he had given up the fight for life. A wave took us off the rocks and I made another attempt to get him out of the water, but this time he was even fighting against me as, again, I struggled to hold my grip. The chance to get him out of the water was lost as yet another wave washed us away.

I scrambled ashore and tied the hawser around my waist, thinking that I could be lifted from the sea while hanging onto the man, but, at that point, the hawser and my fins were discarded by the helicopter as it took off for the New Territories to refuel. I quickly turned my attention back to the Chinese—I couldn't believe it—he was gone, drowned. I was not even sure just where he had disappeared. I dived in, but without a facemask I could see very little and I never set eyes on him again.

My attention quickly turned to the other man. I could not see him from where I was standing so, carrying a spare lifejacket, I set off down the coast. After a few minutes, I noticed his small inflatable pillow; there were no hands clutching it now—he too had disappeared without trace. An army scout helicopter came by, but I paid it little attention. It was not long before I heard the distinctive sound of the Wessex returning. By now, it had been fitted with a winch and it was my pilot, acting as winchman, who came down and picked me up. In a very short time we were above the other craft and it's two occupants were safely winched onboard. I strapped them into their seats and acted reassuringly. Within a couple of months they would probably try again.

CHAPTER FIVE
Fiji
1979

FOR most people, a trip to Hong Kong alone would have been enough, and indeed I was well satisfied, but imagine how I felt when I learned that I was to go to Fiji for two months, and three weeks of that time would be spent teaching diving on a remote tropical island—Makongai. We arrived by boat late one evening in mid-October and it was not until the following morning that I was able to explore, discovering an exciting location ideally suited to our needs.

The island of Makongai has left an indelible impression on me, not least because of its own interesting story. For many years, it was a large leper colony run under the auspices of the World Health Organisation. In fact, the island catered for the needs of two, distinctly separate, leper communities housed only a mile or so from each other. The main group lived in a camp on the shores of a large bay: sheltered by a steep hill to the rear and the adjacent island of Mackondronga, the camp was extremely well sited and protected from the elements all year round. It is possible to fish in that bay whatever the weather.

The second, or Asian, leper community was situated about a mile along the only track on the island. This camp, perched on the shores of the next largest bay on the south of the island, had a rather curious accommodation arrangement; the Asian community lived in brick houses sited amongst the dense coconut trees, whereas the buildings of the main camp, including staff accommodation, theatre and hospital, were out in the open and made almost entirely of wood.

To the north of main camp is a graveyard where many inscriptions and even the occasional photograph on headstones can still be seen. The victims of that dreadful disease, dying so far from home, lie side by side with those who devoted their lives striving to bring some small measure of relief. One such headstone, which bears witness to a lifetime of such dedication, simply reads "In memory of Mother Mary Agnes born France 21.3.1870, died Makongai 17.3.1965 -RIP".

Several of the headstones bear the name Wolfgramm and a plaque on one of the buildings shows that it was once the "Ernest T. P. Wolfgramm Institute". I later discovered that, while there is no absolute cure for leprosy, it was on Makongai that a latter-day Wolfgramm discovered a drug which arrests the spread of the disease. This led directly to the evacuation of leper colonies throughout the world as their importance diminished. Makongai, itself, was evacuated in 1972. The buildings remain intact and well maintained. No real use has been found for them since 1972, although the Fijian Military Forces have used them, as we did, on occasions. The Fijian government is well aware of the island and its potential; however, thoughts of putting the structures to good use are governed by the harsh economic realities of resupplying a remote island. A number of suggestions have been put forward, but a plan to convert the island into a penal colony was fast gaining ground. That just might be the end of the island as I knew it—unspoilt and beautiful.

● A large White-Spotted Puffer Fish (*Arothron Meleagris*). A splendid example of its species.

● An abandoned Hindu Temple amongst the palm trees.

About 50 villagers live permanently on the island, working for the Ministry of Agriculture. The community spirit was incredible. When they fish, they do so for everyone in the village, and when the ladies make reed mats, they make them for every household. They were such a happy group—one big family.

My task was to teach snorkeling and diving to Gurkha soldiers, a challenging and difficult undertaking for several reasons. The Gurkhas have no natural affinity with the sea; in fact, they often see it for the first time when they are on their way to Hong Kong to join up. Certainly they could swim, but there was a distinct lack of knowledge and experience on practically everything to do with the sea—things that we often take for granted.

The prospect of teaching and diving in Fiji came as one of life's more pleasant surprises. Equipped with a locally-hired compressor, six complete sets of diving equipment, and over 30 sets of mask, snorkel and fins, the experience became a cross between a conventional military exercise and an expedition, offering the best of both worlds.

Two reef-forms encircle the island; the barrier reef acts as a massive breakwater out to sea, whilst the fringing reef lies immediately below those waves that lap the shore, providing swimming pool conditions.

I selected a training area some 100 metres long between two old jetties. Walking out on top of the reef for about 20 metres, one came to a point where the coral ended abruptly and dropped two or three metres to the seabed: underwater visibility was exceptional and the sea alive with corals of all description and a myriad of brightly coloured fish. This was my first taste of truly tropical waters and it was breathtaking.

By the end of the first week, I had completed a number of courses and 50 members of the company were competently snorkeling without direct supervision. With that behind me, I turned my attention to the diving and 13 aspiring divers returned to the classroom for further training. We went back to basics, starting again, and over the next few days the numbers dwindled until there were seven left. At this point, a vessel from the Royal Fijian Navy arrived on a resupply run with Leading Seaman John Soro onboard; a most experienced diver, he had trained and dived extensively in Australia. John spent that last week on the island assisting me with the divers and I was glad of his help.

Our biggest diving problem, though not dangerous, was distraction. We were diving in waters that had never seen a diver before and the fish were more curious than frightened. On one occasion, having finished the underwater drills, we were about to surface when I noticed a very large shoal of fish and decided to show my students what it would be like to surface through such a multitude. The centre of the shoal opened up in a lazy fashion as we commenced our ascent—at this point I realised the fish were barracuda! As barracuda go, they were very small, each fish about 18 to 24 inches long; however, I wasn't familiar with the behaviour of this species and I was primarily concerned that one of the students might realise his predicament and panic. I need not have worried. After the dive I explained what had happened to the Gurkhas, but they had no idea what a barracuda was in the first place.....

And so we came to the last day. Deciding to put it to good use, we crossed to the nearby island of Mackondronga where we prepared for a series of shore dives. The pattern for these dives remained the same throughout: John and I entered the water with two students, we then finned out approximately 50 metres from the shore before diving. Keeping together, we dropped to the seabed some 12 metres below and, from there,

● *Below*: A large barracuda: towards the end of one particular dive, we ascended through the middle of a large shoal of barracuda.

● Fijian fisherman with a Spanish Mackerel: such fish were a welcome addition to our diet.

● The divers with the author on the left and Leading Seaman John Soro, Royal Fijian Navy, on the right.

slowly followed the contours of the seabed upwards and back to the starting point, inspecting everything as we went.

It seemed that every dive wanted to reveal something new to us as we encountered turtles, crayfish (one of which provided a meal for no less than seven hungry men), giant clam, grouper and an enormous puffer fish, and collected scorpion shells (*Lambis truncata sebae*) and tiger cowries (*Cypraea tigris*). However, divers the world over are somewhat prone to tunnel-vision: the Gurkhas were so busy looking under a ledge that they completely missed a White-Tipped Shark that John and I were keeping under respectful surveillance.

The time came for us to finally leave the island. Travelling by courtesy of the Royal Fijian Navy, we called in at the ancient capital of Lautoka on our way back to Suva. The following six weeks were taken up with military exercises and the hard work that goes with it. We did manage one more day's diving before leaving for Hong Kong, but it was on a small tourist island which was well dived—there were no shells and most of the coral had been collected. It made me wonder how long it would be, in this ever shrinking world, before Makongai ended up the same way.

CHAPTER SIX
Thailand
1980

TOWARDS the end of our two year stay in Hong Kong, I took my family to Phuket in Thailand for a holiday. We stayed in a small chalet on Patong beach, situated on that remote south-west corner of Thailand, a section of the Malay peninsula bordering the Andaman Sea, itself part of the Bay of Bengal.

The beach was spectacular, a mile and a half of golden sands, ideal for the family. A number of chalets and one large hotel bordered the beach and, although everywhere was fully booked, it was far from crowded. Numerous kiosks along the seafront displayed the usual tourist souvenirs. I was alarmed to see the lengths people would go to in order to produce some saleable trinket from the sea. Apart from the usual configurations made from shells of all sizes, I found preserved hermit crabs still inside their chosen shells; puffer fish lampshades; stuffed angelfish hanging from a piece of string; and even a mobile for a child's bedroom made from preserved butterflyfish.

The fringing reef, lying close to our chalet at the southern end of the beach, was only a metre or so deep at the top but dropped down seven or eight metres in places and provided a home for an exotic collection of tropical fish and invertebrates. I was in the water within an hour of arriving on the beach and out again almost straight away. I had been so preoccupied with taking a photograph that I reached out to steady myself, without looking where I was putting my hand, and was immediately stung on the thumb by a Black Lionfish. I was familiar with the beautiful fish and had even kept one in my aquarium in Hong Kong. I certainly knew them to be poisonous: each of the spines in the dorsal fin, similar in action to a hypodermic syringe, pumps poison through the spine and into the offending object. I now had to find out just how badly I was injured.

It was over an hour before I reached a doctor and by this

time the pain had reached my elbow. The doctor, an American, knew exactly what to do and after treatment I was able to resume my diving with a little more caution and nothing bruised, except my ego.

The nearby reef was rich enough to keep a photographer busy for many years. Numerous fish that were totally new to

● *Left*: A clownfish (*Amphiprion sandaracinos*) and anemone on the fringing reef.

● An aptly named Queen Angelfish, one of the most beautiful and graceful of all marine creatures.

● Numerous starfish inhabited these waters: this blue starfish was found on the fringing reef near to the shore.

me, such as leaf fish, orange-spotted file fish and many more I was unable to identify, swam past my lens. I waited patiently until a profusion of multi-coloured, polymorphous tube-worms, having retracted their fine food-sifting tentacles inside tubular brittle shells attached to the reef, blossomed forth, like a bouquet of flowers, to be captured by my camera.

Whilst diving through this cornucopia of marine life, I met Horst Hinrichs, a German who ran one of two local diving firms called 'Santana Diving'. Having invited me to accompany him on a trip to the Similan Islands, 12 of us departed at the end of the following day on board a small six-berth boat, settling ourselves for a rough night on the open decks, since the journey would take about 10 hours. Woken early the following morning by a crew member who had mysteriously prepared breakfast, it was not long before we were ready for the first dive. However, at this point, I realised something was wrong, we had been at sea for well over 12 hours and there were no islands in sight.

I joined Horst in the wheelhouse, noticing the puzzled expression on his face as he pored over the chart. His English was not too good, but I understood the course he had plotted. I then inspected the compass and immediately spotted the problem: a member of the crew had brought some food packed in an old biscuit tin and had placed the tin right next to the compass. When the tin was removed the needle swung back to the correct position.

Four hours later, we arrived and commenced our first dive below an imposing rock called Neptune's Seat. Splendid underwater scenery confronted us wherever we swam; turtle, barracuda, angelfish and grouper were everywhere and we occasionally saw sharks. On each dive, I used a complete roll of film in a very short time and spent the remainder of the dive admiring the magnificence of the reef. On one occasion we came across a pair of mating cuttlefish, but I had already run out of film. We also spotted a large solitary cuttlefish and surrounded it out of curiosity. Watched by my buddies, I slowly approached and stroked it on the nose; for a brief moment it recoiled from my touch but, to my amazement, came back for more. I couldn't quite believe what was happening—here we were taking it in turns to stroke a cuttlefish and it was behaving like a domestic cat!

After that first dive, we put into the beach on the island of

Goh Minian where we were to spend the next two days. Like the other islands in the Similan group, it was deserted: the sand of finely crushed white coral had a texture like household flour. I was extremely surprised that there wasn't a single palm tree in sight; had I known in advance, I would have brought a coconut husk and set it myself.

The diving during this short visit remained superb. The varieties of fish spotted were too numerous to list, but I do remember a notable lack of moray eels. On one of these dives, I came across a large spiny solarform starfish and subsequently found several more, each a different colour—bright orange, deep purple or dark brown. These were the famous 'Crown of Thorns' Starfish that are reputed to be devastating the Great Barrier Reef in Australia.

During a dive off the island of Goh Pabu, we found a pair of scorpion shells. I remember thinking at the time how we always found these gastropods in pairs in Fiji. However, these waters were curiously lacking in shells so we left them *in situ*. The best diving was reputed to be at Goh Payan, a series of rocks in a straight line, barely breaking the surface. Wary of the treacherous currents around these rocks, we dived on the sheltered side. Here we saw a profusion of multi-coloured lionfish and, for only the briefest moment, a small group of dolphin in the distance. The rocks, large and square-sided like a huge brick wall, were covered with tube-worms and starfish of almost every imaginable species.

On the third and final day we planned a single deep dive on the far side of Goh Pabu, before departing for home. Descending a steep slope, we passed over extensive coral beds until they petered out at about 34 metres—below us, in the distance, we could see some very large grouper, but we were as deep as the dive plan allowed. Commencing a slow ascent across the coral, at 30 metres we came across the anchor; looking up, I saw our craft silhouetted against the sunlight, resembling nothing more than a toy boat. At 10 metres we discovered a captivating coral garden populated by surgeonfish, tang, Emperor Angelfish, octopus, butterflyfish and countless others.

Soon, we were back on the beach, striking camp ready for the return trip. Apart from a few footprints, we left the beach as pristine as we found it. On the return trip, which took all afternoon and part of the evening, we spotted dolphins and flyingfish, but they were never very close. As the journey wore on, everyone grabbed the nearest bar of soap and took advantage of a rain squall to have a much needed shower.

The remaining week at Patong witnessed two interesting developments involving the local authorities. The first incident occurred in shallow water where I was diving with four friends: we came across a cuttlefish and I attempted to stroke its nose as I had done previously. My colleagues and I, giving vent to our curiosity, surrounded the hapless creature. At this point, a Thai spearfisherman swam unseen towards us and shot the cuttlefish. I swear, that spear travelled over my shoulder, missing me by only two or three inches! I was furious. I released the injured cuttlefish and threw the spear gun away into deeper water. The Thai recovered the gun and made for the shore,

● *Below left*: Tube-worms come in a variety of shapes and colours.

● *Left*: A discarded boat. Every seafaring nation has developed its own style of small fishing boat; this craft, originally well made, will have served its' owners well.

● *Below*: A young tropical crayfish, quite a different colour from the adult of the same species.

where I continued to show my disgust at his dangerous behaviour. Believe it or not, it was HE who wished to complain to the Police. His last words to me were—"I am Thai people, you will see". At the time, I dismissed this warning because I was undoubtedly in the right, but I was mistaken.

I was interviewed by the local police and accused of throwing away the speargun, even though it was recovered, and releasing the catch! I described how the incident came about and the dangerous behaviour of the man concerned. At this, the police officer asked to see my injuries. When I pointed out that these were non-existent, he said it proved that, because of the good marksmanship displayed by the spearfisherman, I had obviously been in no danger whatsoever. There was no use arguing and I was fined on the spot. My friends advised me to pay or I might spend weeks in jail without ever seeing a courtroom. I paid the fine and thought that would be the end of the matter, but about a week later I was interviewed again and ordered to pay a further fine. This was to purchase a new speargun for the poor Thai man who had been so cruelly treated by me. Before I left the police station, I watched as the police officer and that unfortunate man shared out the 1,500 Baht that I had paid in fines (£150) between themselves.

The second incident happened on our last evening. We were strolling down the beach when I noticed something floating in the shallow water; too big for a coconut, I wondered if it was a dolphin lying motionless. Suddenly, I realised that I was staring at a human figure floating face down in the water amongst a group of oblivious swimmers. I quickly reached the body, but she had been dead for some time. Jenny went back to the chalet to get a blanket and I asked someone else to fetch the police. A middle-aged Swiss man arrived and identified the body of his mother. Soon, a large crowd had gathered and a friend of the dead lady remained with me while the son went to make various arrangements. A single policeman was present, but made no attempt to take charge of the situation and did not even try to prevent someone removing a ring from the finger of the dead woman.

We were told that the body could not be moved until the doctor had seen it. For three hours we sat on that beach, whilst the family friend repeatedly inquired about the doctor only to be told "doctor take one hour". Totally exasperated, he finally exclaimed, "You keep saying doctor take one hour, why have we been waiting for three hours?" To which the policeman replied, "Ah doctor take one hour from when you go and get him". The son, also exasperated at the lack of real help from the authorities, finally borrowed a Landrover and took his mother to the nearest doctor—I was not even required to make a statement!

It had been a curious trip and had left me with mixed feelings. Certainly the scenery above and below the waves was quite enchanting and often very exciting.

We returned to Hong Kong on January 4th. I immediately posted a few rolls of Kodachrome back to the UK, but I had mainly used Ektachrome and I put twenty-five rolls of this film into a local shop for processing. The laboratory had a small fire and they were all lost—the owners even wanted me to pay for the processing, but that is another story.

CHAPTER SEVEN
Gibraltar
1977 and 1981

GIBRALTAR, that famous bastion of British naval power, offers some of the most advanced diving to be found anywhere in the Mediterranean—most of it is right on the doorstep.

As most people are aware, Gibraltar, guardian of the entrance to the Mediterranean, sits on the southern tip of Spain. It consists of little more than a town, an airport and a dockyard situated around the famous rock. The harbour embraces a naval base at the southern end and a commercial port to the north, each containing a large harbour wall, with an isolated 'centre mole' between the two outer 'moles'. Some of the most

exciting diving is to be found on the seaward side of this 'centre mole'. At one end, an old tug, broken in two, offers a safe haven to all manner of marine creatures; south of this, the old 'cannon site' provides an interesting diversion. The story is told that these piles of old cannon, lying one on top of the other, were once used to defend Gibraltar, but were unceremoniously dumped into the sea when they became obsolete.

HMS Excellent, an old frigate, destroyed during the last war, lies upside down in 20 metres of water close to the cannons. Diving on this wreck is quite an experience. Landing on the upturned hull, the diver can inspect the marine growth at leisure, the more discerning soon following the ship's lines down to the seabed for a more thorough inspection. The propeller is still in place but, before all you 'shiny seekers' go rushing off to remove it, like the cannon and even the 'Albia' in Northern Ireland, it is made of iron.

The engine room is accessible, although it is a tight squeeze and the experience has little to recommend it. For a really exciting dive, turn your back on the engine room, swim right through the upturned hull and out through a break in the bow. It is like a long tunnel dive at night: hanging from the ceiling, a multicoloured mass of sea fans (Gorgonians) appear to await the divers' torchlight to bring them to life and reveal their true colours.

● *Below*: Spanish Dancer. Resembling a creature from outer-space, this nudibranch swims gracefully through the sea in an undulating fashion.

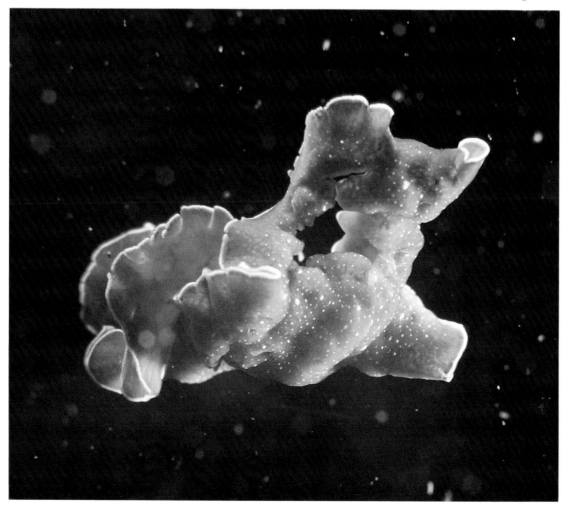

The remains of the 'Roslyn' lie alongside the south mole. A large tramp steamer, wrecked in the early part of the century, she has been a favourite amongst divers for many years. On my first dive, I found two large portholes attached to a bulkhead which had fallen into one of the cargo holds and lain unnoticed ever since. As an exercise in lifting a heavy object from the seabed, we set about removing one of these portholes. After it had been cleaned up we presented it to the Joint Services Diving Club run by Marc who had hosted our visit. That was in 1977 and, when I returned in 1981, I was keen to see if it was still there. It was, and it hung right next to the other one, recovered by another group.

● My diving partner taking photographs on the wreck of the 'Roslyn'.

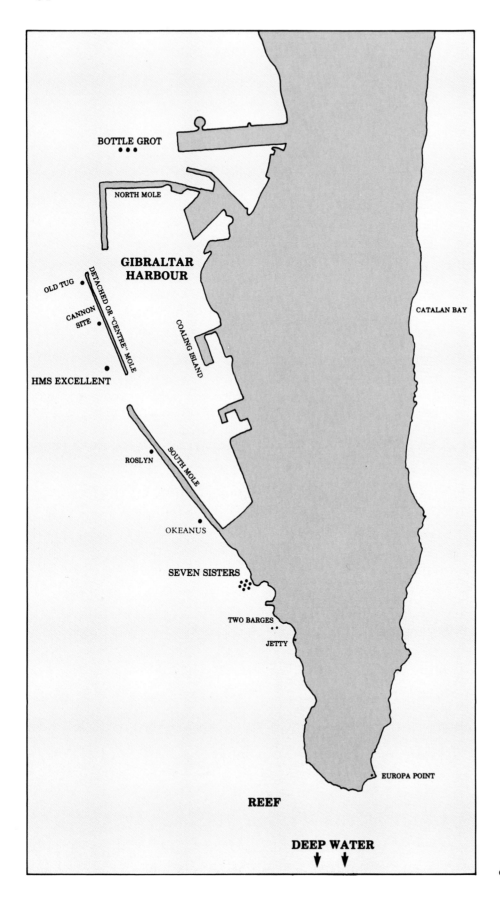

BOTTLE GROT

NORTH MOLE

GIBRALTAR HARBOUR

OLD TUG

DETACHED OR 'CENTRE' MOLE

CANNON SITE

COALING ISLAND

CATALAN BAY

HMS EXCELLENT

ROSLYN

SOUTH MOLE

OKEANUS

SEVEN SISTERS

TWO BARGES

JETTY

EUROPA POINT

REEF

DEEP WATER

● Gibraltar.

Away from the harbour walls, there are several sites worthy of mention. Continuing in a southerly direction, the "Seven Sisters" in Rosia Bay, seven pinnacles of rock jutting out from the sea, provide wonderful opportunities for the photographer; nudibranchs abound and this is the only dive site where I have seen a Spanish Dancer. Our next stop is Camp Bay, an ideal spot for the family and one of the best night-dive sites I have ever found. About 50 metres offshore, two large barges sunk while under tow some years ago: one of the barges rests in an upright position whereas the other, only a few metres away, lies on its side with the dumping doors open. In preparation for a night-dive, we tied a rope to the steps of a small jetty and the other end to one of the barges. We then attached Lumi-sticks along the rope and on top of the barges. Although these glowing sticks were about 10 metres deep, they could be clearly seen from the shore; underwater, the effect was quite eerie, but it did ensure that no-one missed the wrecks in the dark.

Still further south, lies a reef where the water gets very deep indeed. Having set off from the club in its diesel harbour launch, we were over the site in about 20 minutes. At 20 metres, finding nothing but a flat and fairly featureless seabed, we set off in a certain direction and located the reef. It was well worth the effort as we discovered a wonderland of flora and fauna to match anything we had seen so far.

In the other direction, beyond the north mole, there is a dive known simply as the 'Bottle-Grot'. No trip to Gibraltar is complete until the diver has had a successful Bottle-Grot! For many years, Spanish fishermen have rowed their craft up to the buoys that mark the boundary between Spanish and Gibraltar waters. Tying up their boats and dropping fishing-lines, they spend the entire day soaking up the sun and drinking gin. Today, the seabed is littered with glass bottles of the more popular brand names, but it is the earthenware bottles of years gone by that are much sought after by divers. No discerning diver would dare leave Gibraltar without at least one of these old bottles. I remember dive after dive revealing absolutely nothing until the very last one, when we surfaced with no fewer than seven.

I visited Marc at his house and he showed me a collection of over 200 of these bottles. Because each was individually hand-made, no two were identical; however, some brands were more common than others. At that time, Marc was looking for a particular type which he regarded as quite rare. When I returned to Gibraltar in 1981, Marc was working in Germany but had recently visited Gibraltar on a diving trip. The diving club was then run by Rory Wallbanks, who was well known for his sense of humour. Apparently, after years of searching, Marc had found a perfect example of the rare bottle he sought.

● A pair of nudibranch's mating. I only saw three different species of nudibranch in Gibraltar, but each of these was extremely common.

Back at the club, Marc put the bottle safely to one side and was washing down his equipment, when Rory picked up an old cracked bottle and threw it to an accomplice saying, "look what Marc found". Marc was quick to react and ran to catch the bottle, but needless to say it was deliberately mishandled and fell to the ground in a thousand fragments. In a state of total disbelief, Marc began to pick up the pieces until he came across a section which indicated that he was looking at the wrong bottle. Rory was last seen heading for the hills with Marc in full pursuit.

Between these two visits, a new wreck—the 'Okeanus'— appeared in 17 metres of water just out from the Seven Sisters. Fully intact, complete with wheelhouse, funnel and, for the desperate diver, a loo, the tug had apparently sunk within the harbour and John Shirley, another diver from the Centre, arranged to have the vessel towed out to sea and scuttled where divers could easily find it. This is the only time that I have ever heard of the transits being worked out before the wreck went down!

I find the diving in Gibraltar quite exciting. After a day's work club members turn up at the Centre and, having quickly organised a dive, can be on their way home within an hour or two. I can think of no better way to round off a day. At weekends, divers are out in great strength, so that, throughout the year, few days pass without a dive. Personally, I think diving in Gibraltar is far more exciting than many of the more established diving countries elsewhere in the Mediterranean. Certainly one has to contend with currents and tides and, occasionally, the underwater visibility could be better. However, one can dive all year round and visibility is invariably better than we experience in the UK. In short, Gibraltar has a lot to offer.

CHAPTER EIGHT
Northern Ireland
1982, 1983, 1984

JENNY and I, returning to Northern Ireland in 1982, went to live in Portadown. It was near here that our third child Jessica was born in 1983. In the meantime, I had become involved with my old club at Lisburn and eventually took over the reins of diving officer from Dick Champion. The Ulster coastline offers the serious diver some of the finest diving to be found anywhere in British waters. I have, throughout this chapter, selected the more prominent sites; all of these, and many more, were visited by the Lisburn club during my two year stay. Of course, there is no substitute for local knowledge, and I made it my business to meet as many people as possible who were involved with diving in one way or another. In this way, we were able to visit more sites than we would otherwise have known about.

Rathlin is a large island situated above the north-east corner of the province and abounds with good dive sites. However, two particular wrecks are certainly worthy of special attention from the visiting diver—HMS Drake and The 'Lochgarry'.

HMS Drake

A four-funnelled armoured cruiser of 14,000 tons, built at Pembroke dockyard and completed at the turn of the century, HMS Drake was one of the fastest vessels at sea in her heyday but, soon rendered obsolete, was destined to spend the 1914–1918 war in home waters.

HMS Drake was torpedoed whilst protecting an Atlantic convoy. The skipper, Captain Radcliffe, decided to make for Rathlin Island, apparently intent on beaching the stricken ship. However, no sooner had she entered the calm waters of Church Bay, than she began to list at an alarming rate. The ship was abandoned and her complement of 900, including the bodies of the nineteen who lost their lives when the torpedo struck, were taken off. As soon as this was completed, HMS Drake turned over and sank.

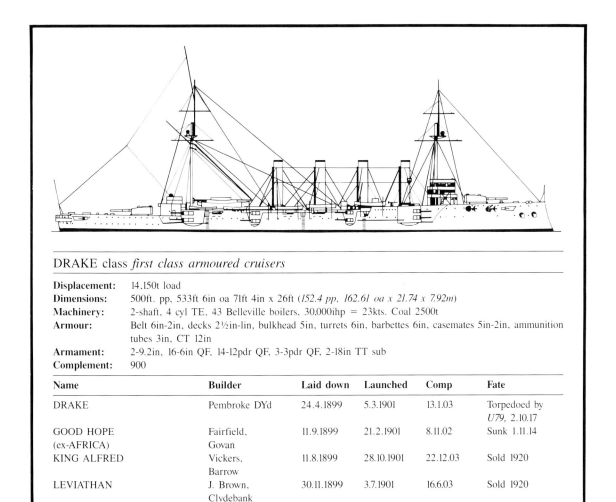

DRAKE class *first class armoured cruisers*

Displacement:	14,150t load
Dimensions:	500ft. pp, 533ft 6in oa 71ft 4in x 26ft (*152.4 pp, 162.61 oa x 21.74 x 7.92m*)
Machinery:	2-shaft, 4 cyl TE, 43 Belleville boilers, 30,000ihp = 23kts. Coal 2500t
Armour:	Belt 6in-2in, decks 2½in-1in, bulkhead 5in, turrets 6in, barbettes 6in, casemates 5in-2in, ammunition tubes 3in, CT 12in
Armament:	2-9.2in, 16-6in QF, 14-12pdr QF, 3-3pdr QF, 2-18in TT sub
Complement:	900

Name	Builder	Laid down	Launched	Comp	Fate
DRAKE	Pembroke DYd	24.4.1899	5.3.1901	13.1.03	Torpedoed by *U79*, 2.10.17
GOOD HOPE (ex-AFRICA)	Fairfield, Govan	11.9.1899	21.2.1901	8.11.02	Sunk 1.11.14
KING ALFRED	Vickers, Barrow	11.8.1899	28.10.1901	22.12.03	Sold 1920
LEVIATHAN	J. Brown, Clydebank	30.11.1899	3.7.1901	16.6.03	Sold 1920

HMS Drake courtesy 'Conway's All the World's Fighting Ships 1860–1905'.

In late 1976, the Royal Navy blasted her apart in order to reduce the danger to surface traffic. Though little of the original vessel is now recognisable, wreckage is spread over a vast area and offers several dives. As the wreckage lies in only 20 metres of water, it is an ideal first wreck dive for the novice diver; however one has to be careful. The wreck is not a war grave and is not unsafe in the sense of high explosives in a dangerous condition, but one must remember that this wreck was once a warship and carried live rounds for her 6 inch, 9.2 inch and 12 pounder guns. These shells can still be found and remain technically 'live', although the pressures that prevail at 20 metres have crushed open each shell-case and over 60 years of salt water have ensured that the shell will remain useless forever.

The 'Lochgarry'

● *Opposite*: Divers ascending from the 'Lochgarry' wreck off the east coast of Rathlin Island.

Lying on the seabed at 30 metres, the 'Lochgarry', is another of those all too rare wrecks, both upright and basically intact. Running aground on 21st January 1942, not on the Ulster coast at all but on the Mull of Kintyre, she drifted helplessly for two days before finally sinking close to the shores of Rathlin Island. Being so deep, like a time-capsule, she remains oblivious and untouched by the storms that come and go with successive winters. Slack water on this part of the coast occurs roughly one hour before low and high tide, and strong currents dictate that this is the only time to visit the wreck. It is at these times that the underwater visibility is exceptionally good.

Taff Jones, coastguard at Portmuck and one of the most genuine guys I have ever met, is deeply involved with the local diving scene in Ulster. In late 1983, I wanted to take a look at a particular site known as the 'Silver Dollar' wreck, having found very little information about it except that silver dollars were for many years washed up on the beach. Taff agreed to come with me and we set off on a bitterly cold day, Taff scoffing at me as I donned my wetsuit–he was wearing a drysuit over a considerable amount of warm clothing. I took my time to dress. Taff was slowly backing into the sea ahead of me when he suddenly screamed, frantically struggled to regain his balance in shallow water, and made the most undignified exit from the sea I have ever seen. He had not zipped up his drysuit, consequently the sea rushed in, drenching him so severely that we had to terminate the dive before we even started. We never did take a look at that wreck–maybe next time.

I described the Maiden Islands in Chapter One; however, at that time I was only able to visit Allen Rock when I dived the 'Albia'. I explored the rest of the dive sites during my later stay in the province. In the early summer of 1983, we found an unidentified wreck, debris stretching from five metres right down to almost forty, at Russell Rock, the outermost of all the Nine Maids. Obviously, the deeper the wreckage the less it is broken up, so the stern section with a few brass portholes is in place and relatively intact. It points upwards at a very steep angle and still manages to hold onto its rudder and propeller (yet another wrought iron propeller!).

● *Left*: Taff Jones ascending from a dive on the Maiden Islands on a day when he remembered to close his zip.

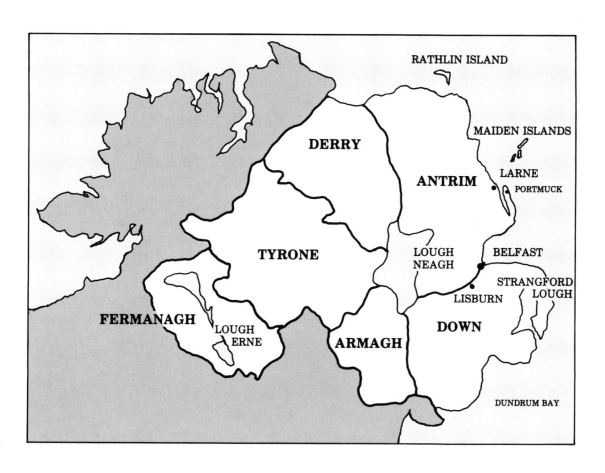

RATHLIN ISLAND

DERRY

MAIDEN ISLANDS

ANTRIM

LARNE
PORTMUCK

TYRONE

LOUGH
NEAGH

BELFAST

STRANGFORD
LOUGH

FERMANAGH

LISBURN

LOUGH
ERNE

ARMAGH

DOWN

DUNDRUM BAY

Several vessels have come to grief on Highland Rock and, as a consequence, wreckage lying there is much confused. The remains of the 'Sumatra' is easily the most distinguishable of all the wrecks. Lost in 1882, she was a brand new square rigger of 1551 tons and quite the largest sailing vessel ever to sink on the east Antrim coast. No longer recognisable as a ship, there is still a lot to see: the wreckage lies in 20 metres on the southern side of the rock in a powerful tide-race that is only completely slack for about 30 minutes, approximately one hour after low and high tide. Dive planning needs to be sharp and the diving officer has to recognise that, once slack water is over, diving must be terminated quickly.

It was off Saddle Rock, just south of the main lighthouse, that the 'Overton', an elderly tramp steamer, foundered in 1955. Although a modern wreck, because of the decrepit nature of the ship, each storm has taken its toll and broken it up a little more. An interesting wreck, but I only caught a brief glimpse of it as we discovered her towards the end of our dive. Wreckage stretches from 20 right down to 40 metres and possibly beyond. I came across a large metal plate sticking up from the seabed and, when I finally looked over it, I was face to face with a big seal. For a split second we stared at each other and then it shot off. I often wonder who got the biggest surprise!

Dangerously concealed beneath the surface, a few miles to the south west and not part of the Maiden Islands, lies Hunters Reef, due east of the Larne ferry terminal. On Christmas Eve 1878, the American liner 'State of Louisiana', inward bound for a cargo of Irish emigrants, fouled the reef and sank a few days later. Now, over 100 years on, she is easily located at 20 metres. Though well broken-up, one can find a surprising number of large pieces of wreckage spread over a vast area: a useful site for introducing the up and coming diver to wreck-diving in conditions not quite as advanced as the Maidens.

Just south of Larne, on the north-east tip of Islandmagee, lies the tiny harbour of Portmuck. Here there is ample room for parking and camping, and the small slipway makes this an ideal base and launching site for diving the Maidens and Hunters Reef. In May 1983, we were diving just to the north of Portmuck; Dick Champion and friend in the water and me following their progress in a twenty-foot dory. Hoping to find some scallops but seeing none, they swam progressively closer to the shore: they had been in the water for about 10 minutes

● *Opposite*: Brian Harrison (Diving Officer, Carrickfergus Sub-Aqua Club) describing the lobster that got away amongst the twisted plates of HMS Drake.

when Dick and his partner surfaced. Bringing the boat alongside quickly, I saw Dick's mouthpiece fall to reveal the biggest grin I have ever seen; handing me a porthole, he said he had "just found a wreck"! With that, I was left on the surface as Dick resumed the dive.

They had discovered the wreck of the 'Rose', a tramp ship which seemed to have spent her maritime career just running aground in one country or another, until she did so once too often in 1892 and became a total loss. To find such a wreck in shallow water—less than 10 metres—was undoubtedly the high light of the year. At this depth, there is no limit to the amount of time that one can spend underwater. Although the wreck had long since undergone salvage, she had been subsequently forgotten by the local diving community. We visited the wreck regularly in May and June and each dive revealed interesting artefacts such as brass portholes and handrails and even a copper steam whistle, all now gracing the Lisburn clubrooms. This site offers the diving officer two great opportunities: not only can he introduce the novice into the fascinating world of wreck-diving but, provided there is no onshore wind, the site is also ideal for introducing the uninitiated to boat-diving (not to be taken for granted when you consider that the best method of

● My colleague, Dick Champion, at Ringhaddy Jetty —about to visit the 'Alisdair'.

entry is for the fully kitted diver to sit on the side of a boat and fall over backwards into the water).

The 'Alisdair', a large motor yacht in 20 metres of water just off Ringhaddy jetty along the western coast of Strangford Lough, is purported to have once once belonged to Messrs Guinness and was commandeered for use during World War Two. What service she actually saw does not appear to be documented but, after the war had ended, she was back at her mooring in front of the jetty, apparently stripped of everything of value by the person placed in charge of her. When a signal was received from the Admiralty to have the vessel prepared for handover to Messrs Guinness, it posed a bit of a problem. The

● At the end of every day in Ulster, a peaceful calm settles over each of the small coastal ports.

76

truth will never be known as the vessel mysteriously caught fire and sank, with surprisingly little damage, at her moorings.

This is a favourite dive for every diver in the province, especially when the weather precludes diving out to sea. The wreck sits upright on the seabed, but underwater visibility is rather poor; and now well silted up, it is no longer possible to actually sit in the bath tub as it was a few years ago. In June 1983, I found an eleven-pound lobster on the wreck which we thought might, quite appropriately, get into the Guinness Book of Records. However, we discovered that another lobster, taken from the same wreck some 10 years previously, had weighed over 14 pounds.

The 'Georgetown Victory', an American Troopship carrying 1200 men of the Royal Navy and Marines home for demobilisation, was a most dramatic, yet inexplicable, wreck. On the night of 30th April 1946 the ship, less than one year old, was 12 miles off her true course for Glasgow when, with a sound of tearing steel that was heard over three miles away, she drove at

● The dramatic wreck of the 'Georgetown Victory'.

full speed onto the rocks of Killard Point, Co. Down. Within a few hours the 'Georgetown Victory' had broken in two, but not before all the passengers had safely disembarked on that fine, calm clear night.

The inquiry was held in camera and the results never published; but why should such a modern ship, on such a calm clear night, simply run aground so far off course? The vessel itself was largely cut up for scrap, but certain parts still remain just to the south of Killard Point and, like all wreck dives, they are so much more interesting when the history of the ship is known.

There are many more sites and wrecks in and around the province; Sunderland flying aircraft lie at the bottom of some of the lakes, and large ships have run aground and disappeared without trace. Diving below the Giants Causeway can be as exciting as the scenery above water. I know of a few British divers who regularly visit Northern Ireland, but many stay away because of the publicity the province earns in the national press. The diving in Ulster is some of the finest to be found anywhere in the world and well worth the visit.

CHAPTER NINE
Cyprus
1983 and 1986

I visited Cyprus for four weeks in 1983 and for three months in 1986 and, whenever I look back on those trips, I think primarily of two men. I went there for two reasons in 1983; firstly, I was to assist the diving centre, based near Dhekelia, in running a diving course; secondly, I wanted to give Jenny and the children a well-earned rest from the pressures of Northern Ireland. So, while I flew to Cyprus by courtesy of the Royal Air Force, Jenny was close behind on a civil flight. My old friend Mal Newman met me on arrival and insisted that we stay with him and his family in their flat. Their hospitality was endless, ensuring that our stay was a complete success.

Long after that holiday, on 1st September 1984, Mal was killed in a fall from his balcony. The world of diving lost a very good diver and I lost a fine friend.

Thoughts of Cyprus also bring Vic Butcher to mind. Vic, the proud possessor of an amazing sense of humour, has been selected for a number of expeditions not only because of his diving skills, but also because of his ability to boost morale at a critical period. Vic, Chief Diver at the Diving Centre, was in Cyprus during both of my visits. He has now left the army and, no doubt, there is a branch of the BSAC somewhere in Lincolnshire benefiting greatly from his membership.

I could probably spend all day telling stories about this man, but a couple of particularly humorous incidents will have to suffice. In 1983, a number of Guardsmen were on the course. Being Guards, they were well-disciplined, standing up and responding 'Sir' every time they were asked a question. As divers, we wanted an 'off-duty' and more relaxed atmosphere but it was difficult to put this message across. Eventually, Vic issued the diving kit while wearing a pair of chimpanzee ears!

All the 'pool-training' was conducted in the sea, so every morning we went to Dhekelia jetty, a large 'Y'-shaped structure that juts out from the beach and is no longer used by boats. Towards the end of that first week, we entered the water with nine students to test what they had learned so far. We swam a short distance and stopped on a clear patch of sand to perform one or two drills before continuing. Never deeper than seven metres, we slowly circled the jetty. As we emerged from the water after an hour or so, we noticed an elderly couple sitting on the beach who had not been there when we commenced our training session. Vic seized the opportunity and, approaching the lady who was watching us intently, asked if this was Cyprus! She replied "yes" whilst furiously pointing inland. Vic thanked her, remarking that it was a long way from Gibraltar and then yelled "come on lads, we're here". Once the laughter was over, I could not help thinking that, somewhere in the world, an old lady regales her friends with the story of the divers who swam from Gibraltar to Cyprus!

The diving is typical of clear, warm, Mediterranean water, but without the vast numbers of fish one finds elsewhere. In fact, the area where we dived is extremely overfished. My first trip was somewhat confined to training, but during my second visit I was based in Nicosia and able to dive almost every week-

end. Three sites stand out in my mind as examples of very good
diving.

The 'Chapel' is so named because the diver gains access to
the dive-site through a large cave below a small chapel on the
rocks nearby. The water here is deep and one can find 30 metres
quite easily, although the best diving occurs between 10 and 20
metres. Many cardinal fish, very small grouper, and a number
of extremely shy soldier fish shelter along a fissure in the rock
on the right-hand side as one descends. The diver can also
locate a number of octopus of various sizes, but I did not see
any signs of crayfish in over 60 dives in Cyprus.

Further round to the left lies a dive site known as the
'Amphora Wreck'—a vast area covered in broken shards of amphorae that were once the cargo of an ancient vessel. There are
no longer any signs of the ship itself and it is also unlikely that
an intact amphora will be found. The earthenware shards have
cemented together over the years, but one can still discover
large pieces which help the diver to recognise what he is looking for.

Amphorae, ancient Greek or Roman earthenware pots with
a pointed base and two elegant handles each side of the neck,
were made in various sizes and used by the trading ships that
once plied these waters. The ships were fitted out with a hori-
zontal beam containing holes in which the pointed bases sat,
the neck secured with rope or other fitting, so that the pot
remained immobile during the voyage. The larger amphorae
contained bales of expensive cloth and the smaller ones spices
and such like.

Another quite interesting dive site, not far from the
'Chapel' is known as 'Tunnels and Caves'. The fully-kitted diver can walk out to a small headland and enter the water above
a large cave. Because it is so shallow the cave itself is of little
interest, but further along, as the diver works progressively
deeper, one finds a number of interesting caves and swim-
throughs. However, the highlight of this dive comes as one
leaves the water. The diver enters a larger cave, which has a
long narrow entrance, and well inside the cave he can see a
number of small holes through which he can quickly and
cleanly leave the water.

Cyprus is very short of wrecks, but closer to Dhekelia there
is a quite exciting one lying upside down in approximately 30
metres. She is a rather curious shape, being extremely flat and

wide. Some of the divers at the Dhekelia club, having done some research, have come up with the theory that she was once used on the river Nile. One thing is certain, she was once a proud vessel with deck timbers of the finest wood and portholes all made of brass. Even now, she is still a fine sight as a multitude of fish mill round her.

I was approaching the end of my dive on the 'Ormedia' when I noticed that Vic was not wearing his knife. I assumed he had just lost it and thought we could spend a moment or two searching for it. I pointed this out to him silently and, although puzzled for a moment, he soon understood what I was trying to say, but his reply had me totally baffled. In three separate movements, he placed his left hand over his left eye, left breast and left buttock. I looked suitably puzzled and he repeated the gesture more slowly. At this point, we dismissed the idea and surfaced. Later, back onboard the boat, I tackled him and, explaining that I thought he had lost his knife during the dive, I asked him what the gestures meant. "Simple", he replied, "I left it behind". I have yet to see that hand-signal published in the diving manuals although, since then, I have used it myself many times.

Finally, the jetty itself at Dhekelia–not a dive site you would travel a long way to visit, but one which does have its interesting facets: on one single dive we saw a Golden Moray Eel, a common moray, octopus swimming in the open and a very large grouper–all at a time when I had left the camera behind! Underneath, the jetty is breaking up and the fractured pieces create niches for a number of creatures. Sea urchins and bristle worms abound here and can both be a bit of a nuisance: bristle worms have bristles all along the sides of their body and, if these come into contact with the skin, they can be quite painful. The jetty pillars are coloured red with a variety of algae and red cardinal fish and small blue damselfish dart in and out of every crevice. We occasionally saw four barracuda; they were not particularly large but often visited the jetty to feed. All in all quite a paradise for the photographer and biologist.

There is no doubt that Cyprus, with its climate and clear water, could very easily be turned into a major resort for sports diving; but firstly, like Hong Kong, there must be some control of overfishing. With an increased fish population, a few well-placed wrecks would be the icing on the cake.

● *Above*: Tube-worm.

● *Opposite*: Divers underneath the Jetty at Dhekelia. This jetty is a haven for numerous small creatures; we even found a Golden Moray Eel on one occasion.

● Paul Almond on 'Amphora wreck', 'Chapel' Cyprus.

● Divers
examining a rock
near Dhekelia jetty.

CHAPTER TEN
Chief Diver, Operation Raleigh
1985

I remember looking back over the furious water created by the twin outboard motors and watching as the 'Sir Walter Raleigh', my home for eight months, grew gradually smaller. In that short time we had visited nine British ports, the Channel Islands, New York, North Carolina, the Bahamas, the Turks and Caicos Islands, Miami, Tampa, New Orleans, Houston, Belize and finally La Ceiba and Roatan in the Honduras. The ship was then at anchor off Black River and I was moving on.

Operation Raleigh, a four year, round the world series of three month expeditions, is aimed at promoting leadership qualities and a better understanding between young people of different nationalities. These young Venturers, 17–24 years of age, participate in a programme run under the Patronage of His Royal Highness, The Prince of Wales, who takes a close interest in the operation, and the direction of one of the British Army's best known and most colourful characters–Colonel John Blashford Snell MBE (known to everybody as JBS).

It was JBS who appointed me Chief Diver and thrust me headlong into an organisation still desperately trying to raise the necessary cash to bring all their plans to fruition. Four thousand Venturers from all over the world were due to take part in Operation Raleigh, in addition, there were experienced Volunteer Staff to take charge of the Venturers in the field. It was certainly no holiday; the Venturers undertook serious scientific, archaeological, medical, community welfare and adventurous tasks. On the diving side, these included a variety of projects while visiting underwater caves, reefs and wrecks. Some of the more exciting 'non-diving' exploits included surviving in jungles, trekking across deserts with camels, sailing the 'Zebu', and climbing mountains in Tibet rarely made accessible to anyone from the western world.

A number of vessels joined Operation Raleigh from time to time, but two ships were to remain for the entire four years; the 'Sir Walter Raleigh' and the square-rigged brigantine 'Zebu'. The 'Sir Walter Raleigh', a 1900 ton former North Sea trawler, was originally adapted for research work in the North Sea oil fields before her conversion for use on Operation Raleigh.

● The square rigged brigantine 'Zebu'. The only vessel, apart from the flagship, to take part in the operation for the entire four years.

She is equipped with:
  Operations Room.
  Communications Centre.
  Exhibition Deck.
  Large Storage Hold.
  Three Scientific Laboratories.
  Fully-equipped Workshop.
  Kitchen and Canteen.
  British Pub.
  Administrative Office.
  Darkroom.
  Diving Store.
  Surgery.
  Computer Room.
  Shop.
  Laundry.
  Upper Boat Deck
  (holding two Avon Seariders and four Skiffs)
  After Boat Deck
  (holding two large, flat-bottomed, landing craft).

● 'Sir Walter Raleigh' waiting to sail up the Mississippi.

The highlight of my time with the operation was, of course, the extensive diving programme during the first phase. At the beginning, I was assisted by Bob Estridge and Charles Hastie and later, Eric Niemi joined us. I think I can safely say that we formed a formidable team.

In just under three months we completed no less than 3,800 dives involving over 200 divers (although there were only 80 to 90 divers at any one time). Most of the Venturers were only taught to dive immediately prior to joining us in the Bahamas, making initial progress slow. By way of supporting Operation Raleigh, the BSAC had agreed to train prospective Venturers in the four year period. It is to the eternal credit of those BSAC instructors, and our own small but experienced group of divers, that there were no accidents or incidents of any kind during that massive diving programme.

The actual diving projects included surveying the world famous Blue Holes, Reefwatch, seagrass mapping and searching for 16th century wrecks.

The Blue Holes

The Blue Holes are a series of caves and large caverns formed above sea-level but now lying submerged, offering exciting and advanced diving in an environment of stalactites and stalagmites rarely seen underwater.

'Ben's Cave' in the Lucayan National Park, near Freeport, on Grand Bahama Island is one of the better known cave-dives. It is comprised of a large hole in the ground, created by the collapse of the cave ceiling many years ago. From here there is a 20 foot drop to a large rock pool surrounding the fallen rock on which the visitor may stand.

On the day I dived 'Ben's Cave', the Canadian TV company 'CTV' were filming us for a show entitled 'Thrill of a Lifetime'. Bright sunshine channelled through that hole, 20 feet above, to create a shaft of light 'through which we travelled on our way to an enormous underwater cavern—a cathedral carved by nature where only the privileged few can come to pay homage. Despite the paucity of flora and fauna, which so enhance any underwater exploration, I found myself spellbound with the beauty of this place. I could now understand the mesmerising attractions of cave-diving.

Reefwatch

The Reefwatch programme was very popular with the Venturers, giving them an appreciation and genuine interest in the weird and wonderful creatures they were constantly encountering underwater. It is an extensive worldwide programme aimed at protecting the world's underwater environment, is run by York University, and Operation Raleigh is only one means currently employed to carry out the work involved. Essentially a data-collecting exercise, the more complex work is carried out in laboratories at a later date. Divers followed carefully laid transects down to 20 metres, recording specific information as they went. Those Venturers involved with Reefwatch will be better divers and possess a greater understanding of the underwater environment because of that involvement.

Seagrass Mapping

Seagrass mapping in itself, was not a particularly exciting project; however, it was potentially the most important from the viewpoint of the Bahamian government. Seagrass, growing in shallow sandy areas and resembling an underwater lawn of thick-bladed grass, is the staple diet of turtles and conch (pronounced conk) shells. Turtle numbers throughout the world are declining and the conch is a local industry in its own right, providing work for many people who farm this shellfish. The project was run by Dr Anitra Thorharg, an American, who featured in The National Geographic on this subject.

Diving from 'Zebu'

Although also used for sail training, the 'Zebu' doubled as the diving base of a team searching for ancient wrecks.

South of the Caicos banks lies the Molasses Reef and it was along this, normally inaccessible, reef that Venturers enjoyed the finest diving of the entire first phase. Such an exciting and unspoilt spot must rival anywhere in the world as a diving location.

When the Spanish Galleons of old crossed the Caribbean on their way back to Spain, loaded to the gunwhales with treasures from Central America, they would pass close to Jamaica and then sail between Cuba and Haiti. Those skilled enough to have survived this far now encountered the Caicos Banks and here any deviation from a true course brought them to grief on Molasses Reef.

Although no finds of startling importance were discovered, the divers did locate 12 wrecks identified by ballast stones, cannon balls and the occasional ancient timber.

During this first phase, I came across one young man who is undoubtedly the bravest I have ever met. Robert Jones, hailing from Plymouth, suffers from cerebral palsy. Many people make the mistake of speaking to Robert as though they were addressing a partially deaf five-year-old, but Robert soon puts them straight. Behind that fumbling exterior lies one of the sharpest minds and a determination to win that can bring him only success. I have seen this man tackle rock-climbing and yachting; he even crewed Robin Knox-Johnstone's 'British Airways II' from Jamaica to the Bahamas. On Operation Raleigh he worked as hard, if not harder, than his able-bodied counterparts and, whenever we put into port, I looked forward to seeing him again.

Returning to Nassau one afternoon, Robert was on the quayside as we docked. I invited him in for a drink and, as we sat and chatted in my cabin, he noticed a 'girlie' calendar on the wall. With great effort he said how he liked the calendar, so I attempted to give it to him, explaining that I never used it and if he wanted it he could take it. He replied in his typically humorous vein, "No thanks, I'll go blind and I have enough problems".

● A Venturer working on the 'Reefwatch' project.

● The divers of
Operation Raleigh.

Off-duty diving

It would have been negligent to confine the diving solely to project work. We were in the midst of some very fine diving locations and it was up to us to take full advantage of that. No doubt each diver will remember a particular dive which was important to them; personally I completed over 130 dives and, of all the locations I visited, it would be hard to determine which was the best.

On four occasions we visited a reef just off the main jetty on Grand Turk Island. Two of these dives were at night and, on the second, we came face to face with a five foot barracuda. Using a trick, learned in my early days in the country, we kept a torchlight on the eye of the barracuda at all times; this worries the fish to the extent that it is unable to move and therefore presents a sitting target for the underwater photographer. My partner, Charles Hastie, kept the light on the fish's eye throughout this brief encounter, enabling me to take several photographs before the fish became suddenly startled and disappeared into the dark sea.

Working with Canadian Television, we had a most exciting week's diving with spectacular night-dives, wreck-dives, another visit to the Lucayan Caves and, would you believe, hand-feeding Bull Sharks.

The wreck-dive centred on a visit to 'Theo's Wreck', named after the man who arranged the sinking of a large bulk carrier as a diving attraction in 1983. Lying on her port side, the starboard side is about 20 metres from the surface and 30 metres to the seabed.

We descended the anchor line and swam slowly to the stern of the ship: the propeller and rudder are in place and even the radar scanner still revolves. She lies pointing towards the shore and beyond the stern are the very deep waters of the continental shelf. All too briefly the dive was over and we were heading back to the surface, but not before we caught a glimpse of a Spotted Eagle Ray flying through the water. These large rays swim by moving the sides of their body up and down like a large bird caught in slow motion.

Then I was whisked away to Stella Maris on Long Island where I met George Friese. George, one of the few people in the entire world who can guarantee sharks at any time, has lived in Stella Maris for over 20 years and runs a hotel and marina.

During that time he has give all the main reefs a name–names such as Angelfish Reef, Flamingo-tongue and Shark Reef vividly describe what the diver will find. After collecting some bait, we anchored above Shark Reef.

The water was perfectly clear and only 11 metres deep: George held a long spear with a dead fish on the end and a Bull Shark appeared almost immediately. Each time a shark took the bait, it would chew, swallow and quickly return to the spear for more. George was ready for this and each time prodded the beast away with the point of the spear. This enabled him to remain firmly in charge of the feeding and not allow it to get out of hand and develop into a feeding frenzy. On one occasion, a shark returned to the spear so quickly that George was not ready and missed it. The shark kept coming; first it was kicked by George and then I thumped it. Another shark took bait and spear and, when the spear was recovered, it was very bent indeed. Still undeterred by all this, a young Venturer, Lisa Walker was at last handed the spear and fed the sharks herself. Then the sharks started to disappear, although one or two did hang around for quite some time. We surfaced and Lisa was clearly pleased it was all over.

I, however, was not quite finished. Here was a golden opportunity to take more photographs and I was soon back in the water with Robin Cass. We stood on the seabed and I discovered that clicking the fingers attracted the sharks; in no time they were passing between Robin and myself as I took photographs.

I have seen sharks in Fiji, Thailand and Hong Kong and, invariably, they have been the source of exciting encounters. During the filming in Stella Maris, I can only say that I have never been so enthralled for such a long period of time, but remember this–there is no such animal as a tame shark. Sharks are wild, ruthless, unpredictable and hungry—always hungry.

With the first phase successfully completed, we set sail for the USA where the Venturers left the operation and flew home. We then commenced a promotional tour of the USA, visiting Miami, Tampa, New Orleans and Houston before crossing the Gulf of Mexico and beginning the second phase.

Phase Two involved such countries as Belize, Costa Rica, Panama, Honduras and the island of Roatan to the north of Honduras. It was here that I left the 'Sir Walter Raleigh' and

● A Bull Shark
of Stella Maris.

● Marina Ogilvy
studying coral
formations—Roatan,
Honduras.

● Cave diver; Photo
by Mark Vinall.

joined the divers on Roatan for my last three weeks before returning to civilisation.

An excellent reef, along which we regularly dived not far from the camp, has one spectacular spot known as 'The Hole in the Wall'. The diver, descending through a hole in the seabed, swims through a tunnel created by overhanging coral and, following this short tunnel, continues to descend, finally exiting on the vertical wall of the reef face.

We regularly showed the Venturers this site, including the tunnel through which they followed their leader in a single file. On one occasion, we were approaching the hole when one of the Venturers looked down through the coral and called me back. Sitting on the floor of the tunnel was a 12-foot Nurse Shark! I made it quite clear that we were still continuing with the dive, each of the divers acknowledging my signal. Setting the camera, I headed off. I approached the shark very slowly, but it became startled, turned and swam away. I turned to check on the divers and found myself in the tunnel alone—they were all watching from above the coral!

On another occasion, we hired a small boat and set off for three days to the north west tip of the island. Again we saw Bull Sharks, large crayfish and one big turtle which came quite close before becoming frightened. Here we dived to 40 metres, the deepest I had been since that trip to Monte Cristo in 1977.

Undoubtedly a completely successful trip and one which will be hard to follow; although, given time, I am sure JBS will come up with something. I consider it a privilege to have been able to take part and I am proud of what was achieved.

CHAPTER ELEVEN
Belize
1987

IN early 1987 I was commissioned, promoted to the rank of Captain and posted to 2nd Battalion The Parachute Regiment as Paymaster (I must have been doing something right!). I was quite excited about returning to a unit with which I had served as a corporal. But more importantly, by October of that year the entire battalion was serving in Belize, Central America, on a six month tour of duty.

● An aerial view of the famous Blue Hole. This is the largest Blue Hole in the world and the only one, to my knowledge, which is large enough to take a ship at anchor.

I was quick to realise the potential of such a trip and I knew it would not be long before soldiers of all ranks would be asking to learn to dive. We obtained some equipment and formed a new branch of the BSAC. I also purchased my own boat and had it fitted with twin Mariner outboard motors. We had used these engines exclusively on Operation Raleigh and I wanted an outboard on which I could rely. It proved to be a good choice; on seeing my boat the battalion purchased one that was identical. So we arrived in Belize with two good diving boats, two compressors and 26 sets of diving equipment: in addition many of the divers had their own equipment.

We were based at Airport Camp, which is not far from Belize City. The other camps in the south had less facilities than ours, so it was here that we concentrated the bulk of the diving equipment and the expertise. Kevin Carter and Steve Thayer set up a training school on Hunting Cay (pronounced Key): their job was to teach diving as a full time occupation. Each week six students would fly out to the Cay and replace the previous batch. They worked very hard and it all went well with no mishaps and plenty of sound instruction and exciting diving.

Meanwhile, in the north, I had a full time job as Paymaster so my approach had to be slightly different. I began by teaching diving on two evenings each week, taking these novices out at weekends for practical training in the sea. It started slowly, but as soon as one or two of the participants spoke to their friends about what they had seen underwater, the club began to grow at a healthy rate. We were soon in full swing and diving regularly every weekend.

Belize City

The Belize river runs close to Airport Camp and this is where we regularly launched our boat—several miles inland. We had two options: either we stay with the river and travel through Belize City, or take a detour and run straight out to sea through shallow waters containing numerous hazards such as sunken trees and sandbanks. Travelling through Belize City also had its problems although these were not as obvious as the water obstacles.

A lot of Belize City can only be described as shanty town; the people are poor and the housing is quite inadequate. Be-

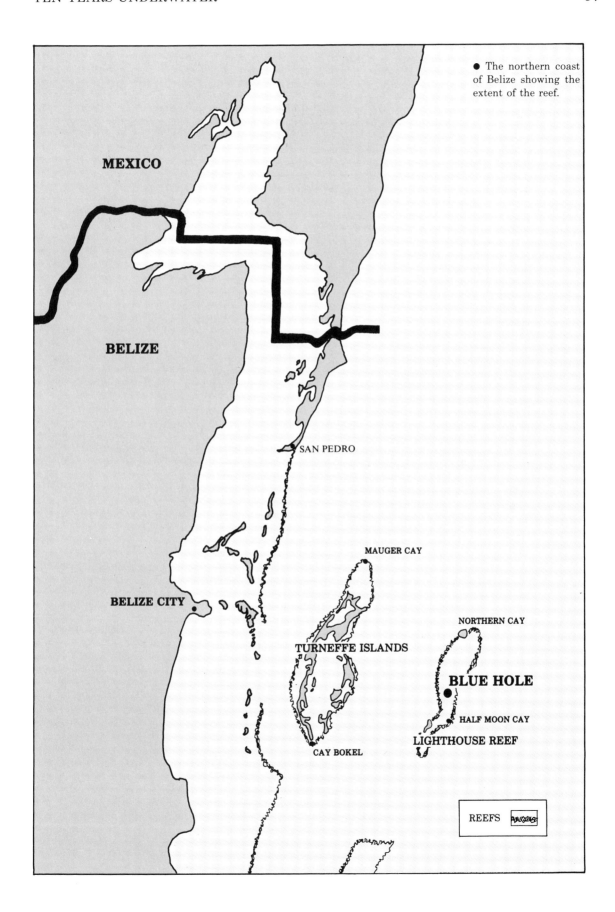

● The northern coast of Belize showing the extent of the reef.

MEXICO

BELIZE

SAN PEDRO

MAUGER CAY

BELIZE CITY

NORTHERN CAY

TURNEFFE ISLANDS

BLUE HOLE

HALF MOON CAY

CAY BOKEL

LIGHTHOUSE REEF

REEFS

cause the dwellings do not have any form of sanitation except for, perhaps, a hole in the floor, all the raw human sewage, totally untreated, finds its way into the river as it runs through the city en route to the sea. As a result, the Belize River has developed its own distinctive dark brown hue. From early morning, every morning, as the dark brown waters run out to sea, this brown patch of pollution spreads an ever widening trace at the mouth of the river. By late afternoon the stain is well out to sea but, fortunately, the reef is still a few more miles further to the east.

In the city, right next to the river, is the large green fish market building. Almost every day big turtles, still very much

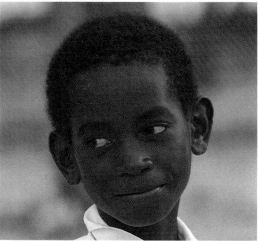

● South of Half
Moon Cay the reef is
particularly beautiful
with breaks in the
reef providing the
diver with exciting
and colourful 'swim
throughs'.

Opposite page:
● *Left*: A local boy
from San Pedro.

● *Far Left*: By
contrast, the shallow
dives inside the Blue
Hole were of little
interest. The
profusion of coral
that exists elsewhere
in this region does
not form inside the
Blue Hole.

● *Below*: Drying
fishing nets—Belize
City.

alive, can be found lying on their backs awaiting their fate. The head of a large Green Turtle is about the same as that of a human being and, as I stood and watched, one of them sighed— it was no more than a deep breath as these creatures can survive both in and out of the water. It is very sad to watch such a proud creature suffer, yet lying on its back with front flippers tied together is nothing compared to the agony that awaits this hapless animal. There is no refrigeration in this fish market and, on those days when the temperature soars, keeping food fresh until it is sold can be a serious problem. One fisherman dispassionately described to me how he kept his turtle meat fresh despite the heat. "It was simple", he said, "you do not kill the turtle, you continue to serve the customers by cutting off exactly the amount of meat required until the creature dies. Then you sell off the remainder quickly"!

One phenomenon worthy of mention is that nature has developed a sewage disposal system of its own. A certain breed of catfish has evolved that generally feeds on pollutants and it is illegal to remove these fish from the river. Whenever fishermen throw scraps and waste into the water, it momentarily boils with the writhing bodies of these catfish as they greedily devour the food, bearing a marked resemblance to a shoal of Piranha attacking some small creature.

Many people travel to Belize for a holiday. Though few would wish to stay in the city, there are numerous other attractions. A Jaguar Reserve was recently opened by His Royal Highness, Prince Philip. Many other rare indigenous animals are, like the Jaguar, protected by law: Manatee inhabit the rivers as well as crocodiles (there are no alligators); pythons can be found amongst the mangroves; and the brightly coloured Belizean-Blue Butterfly often fluttered by as we sped along the river on our way out to sea. Belize is also an ornithologists' paradise; brilliantly plumaged birds compete in colour and form with the most exotic of tropical fish; storks, ibis, toucans and the smaller, brightly coloured finches are present in large numbers. How often did we sit down to an early morning coffee on the verandah and quietly watch as a delicate humming bird flitted from flower to flower only a few feet away, hovering at each bloom before moving on. However, the wildlife that I and many others in Belize seek is to be found underwater. Belize City is eight miles west of the reef and the sea is a great diluter. In other words there is a lot of water between the city and the reef, and the reef, so far, remains unaffected by pollution.

The barrier reef

The second largest barrier reef in the world starts north of Belize at Xcalak in Mexico. Reefs occur further north, but since there are breaks in this system these are considered as separate entities. The barrier reef stretches south for 200 miles before ending at Hunting Cay. We were able to dive on both the northern and southern extremities of the reef as well as numerous sites in between. In addition, there are three islands, or Atoll Reefs, to the east of the main reef: Glovers Reef, Turneffe Island and Lighthouse Reef. There are only seven Atoll Reefs in the entire Caribbean.

Almost everyone knows that the 'Great Barrier Reef' is situated off the coast of Australia. However, the term 'barrier reef' is a morphological one describing a type of reef that may be found anywhere; for example, almost every island in Fiji is surrounded by its own barrier reef. The barrier reef in Belize is like a gigantic underwater brick wall, running parallel to the coast. West of the reef are shallow sandy waters with numerous small islands and cays and, to the east, stretch the deep waters of the Caribbean. Glovers Reef, Turneffe Island and Lighthouse Reef are like blocks of barrier reef rising up out of the depths of the sea with the deeper water outside the reef and shallow, sandy waters within. To the east of these islands there is nothing but a vast expanse of sea.

The Great Blue Hole

In the centre of Lighthouse Reef there is a large and almost perfectly circular hole. Here the water is 408 feet deep, whereas elsewhere within the reef it is only 10 to 15 feet deep. It is the depth of water, like the deep water that surrounds the reef itself, which gives rise to the very dark blue colour and therefore the name of Blue Hole. In 1972 that great pioneer of diving, Jacques Cousteau, took his famous research ship, Calypso, into the Blue Hole and, even though its existence was known beforehand, Jacques Cousteau discovered the Blue Hole of Belize.

● An experimental
picture of the divers
amongst the
wreckage on Banco
Chinchorro using
Infra Red film.

Every diver visiting Belize is keen to dive the Blue Hole and put it into his logbook. When you understand what the hole is and how it was formed you will understand why. The Blue Hole was once an underground cavern forming the centre of an underground cave complex—some of the caves are thought to be linked right through to the mainland. At some time in the distant past, two distinct events occurred. Firstly, there was a major disturbance of the earth's surface—most likely an earthquake—which probably caused the cavern ceiling to collapse. This upheaval also had the effect of tilting Lighthouse Reef over at an angle of approximately 13 degrees, for along the walls of the Blue Hole are overhangs and ledges housing stalactites, stalagmites and columns; with some of the stalactites now hanging at an angle of 12 to 13 degrees—yet a stalactite cannot form at any angle other than perfectly perpendicular.

The second event was the melting of the glaciers at the end of the great Ice Age. It would appear, however, that this did not happen in one big 'melt down'; instead the melting was completed in stages with lengthy breaks between each stage. The evidence for this is in the shelves and ledges, found at various depths running the complete circumference of the hole. The first of these ledges occurs at 150 to 160 feet on the south side of the hole. There are, of course, stalactites that are perfectly perpendicular and were therefore formed after the 'earthquakes'; others appear to have been formed both before and after that cataclysmic event, with the top of the stalactite being at an angle and the bottom perpendicular.

Diving the Blue Hole is not for beginners. Of course anyone can put their head under the surface and claim to have dived the site, but they will have seen nothing. The deeper one dives in the Blue Hole, the clearer the water and the more exciting the terrain. There are blue holes in the Bahamas and elsewhere in the Caribbean, but the one in Belize is the only blue hole that can be seen from space. I believe it should be renamed 'The Great Blue Hole'.

Our divers' progress

We soon got to know the water hazards and the best routes out to the reef and the divers continued to learn at a steady pace.

After several weekends of training drills we became steadily more adventurous. However, the lack of a recompression chamber in Belize has led to a major restriction on all service diving clubs: we were limited to a depth of 30 metres. Initially this was not a problem as all divers must learn to walk before they can run and, therefore, the deeper diving must come at a later stage in the training.

It may be difficult for the non-diver to understand what I mean by the impression of depth. In British seas, the water gets colder and darker with depth. In a climate like that of Belize, where air and sea temperatures allow diving all year round, the clear underwater visibility reduces the impression of depth and it would be easy for the novice to stray over the line and remain too deep for too long. Sound instruction coupled with good training are now at the forefront of all dive planning—'Plan the dive and dive the Plan'. As training progresses, divers will always seek the next horizon. It is more desirable that those horizons can be achieved under sound progressive instruction rather than denied altogether. I tried every means of obtaining permission to go beyond 30 metres before the end of my time in Belize and I came very close. But in the final analysis, the phenomenon of the Blue Hole and other deep underwater sites were denied to my novice divers.

We discovered a small man-made island where a native fisherman lived with his two dogs—Whitey and Brownie—and we became regular visitors. On arrival we unloaded our surplus kit, spare cylinders, food and drinks and departed on the first dive of the day. When we returned, the fisherman would have the bar-b-que ready. Each time we visited, we gave him some cigarettes and a few cold beers; he also had a good lunch. I well remember when we first visited the island how fierce the dogs appeared to be but, after a few weekends, they too were pleased to see us—they also had a good meal that day.

From this island we visited a section of the reef called Gallows Point Reef. Not an endearing name and hardly a site for any gallows, but the diving was quite extraordinary. If anything, I am a very enthusiastic diver and the one thing that continually fires that enthusiasm is the joy of seeing something underwater for the first time. On one occasion we were completing a series of training dives where I, as the only instructor, dived with each student, one at a time. Each time I returned to the boat, I hung on to the side as the students changed over.

Suspended in the water, I looked down as the most graceful of all marine creatures, the giant Manta Ray, glided past right beneath me. Later, on a similar occasion, we saw numerous large Spotted Eagle Rays. These fish do not swim through the water, they 'fly' in slow motion with a grace and magnificence rarely seen elsewhere.

All the way down to 30 metres, we were looking at a rich, healthy and abundant reef. Every now and then, amongst the Staghorn and Elkhorn Corals, we found an outcrop covered in Sea Fans. Everywhere there was a myriad of colourful fish with species too numerous to mention. Spotted Eagle Rays and large Sting Rays became commonplace. Nurse Sharks were often present, but were elusive when it came to photography. Angelfish, butterflyfish, barracuda, squirrelfish, hamlets, basslets, grunts and groupers abounded, to name but a few. We did occasionally see a turtle underwater, but they are shy creatures and were soon out of sight. The larger fish are found in the deeper waters of the 'drop off', which is a feature of the reef. On one occasion, we saw an Oceanic White-Tip Shark with its attendant Pilotfish. This was another 'first' as these particular sharks rarely, if ever, approach the shore.

By the end of 1987, we had enjoyed three months of some of the best diving to be found anywhere in the world. The trainees had gained their first BSAC qualifications and I felt that the time had come for something more adventurous. I planned three expeditions for 1988, each of which was to be more progressive than its predecessor. I labelled them Exercise 'Eagle Ray', 'Manta Ray' and 'Lone Shark'—quite an appropriate name being the Paymaster! To begin with, the time had come to dive the Blue Hole.

● Queen Triggerfish.

● Four Amberjacks.

● *Below*: Four large
Spotted Eagle Rays
seen in the distance.
Although this
particular fish was
very common, they
were also extremely
shy and thus proved
difficult to
photograph.

Exercise 'Eagle Ray'

I booked one of the army's landing craft and we sailed for Half
Moon Cay on New Year's Day. There were 22 divers in the
party and the weather was really atrocious. Half Moon Cay,
the only inhabitable island within this reef, is situated at the
south-east corner of Lighthouse Reef. It is an idyllic spot occupied only by John Lalandby, the lighthouse keeper, and his
family. Half of the Cay is a bird sanctuary, Booby and Frigate
Birds being the most common occupants, but the remainder of
the Cay is less densely overgrown with plenty of room for tents
amongst the coconut trees.

The landing craft was able to drop its bow door right on the
beach making unloading simple, especially as I had brought
along my boat on its trailer. We completed the first dive with
difficulty as the weather was worsening. We dived on the west
side of the reef to the north of Long Cay—a spectacular 'drop
off' that appears to go down forever. However, getting back to
the Cay was a tortuous journey as the seas had become quite
rough.

Chart 959 clearly shows two wrecks on the east of the reef
close to Half Moon Cay. The nearest of these is a large tramp
steamer sitting right up on the top of the reef; the second was
about five miles further north and almost out of sight. Directions for the Blue Hole stated that we should travel to the
second wreck and then steer 310 degrees until a white post
indicated the entrance to the hole.

We followed these instructions carefully and we could see
a yacht anchored in the distance. 'Smudge' Smith turned to me
as we searched for the hole and said "I bet that yacht is anchored over the Blue Hole". I said that this was impossible, it
was a long way off course. After another 30 minutes of fruitless
searching, I turned to 'Smudge' and said "I bet that yacht is
anchored over the Blue Hole". It was—our directions were
wrong by 20 degrees and should have read 330 degrees from the
second wreck. Nevertheless, we had found the famous Blue
Hole and quickly returned to camp and collected the first of the
teams to dive it. This was, after all, the objective. There was
enough time for two of the four teams to dive the site on the
Saturday and the remainder to do so on the Sunday. Belize has
fickle weather at times and Sunday dawned clear and sunny,
enabling the divers to see far more because of the increased

underwater visibility. The last of the groups actually saw a 10 foot Hammerhead Shark, which followed them before disappearing into the depths. I thought this might be a good opportunity to get a photograph of such a shark, but I failed to convince my team of the merits of a second dive after the shark had been sighted.

Traversing the Blue Hole at 30 metres allows only a 20 minute dive before commencing to surface. There is very little life inside this hole carved out of limestone by the rainstorms of countless millions of years ago. The reef 'drop-offs' that I have referred to are equally as steep-sided yet abound with coral. Here it is bare rock and this puzzled me. I have now come to the conclusion that the lack of flora and fauna in the Blue Hole is directly related to the lack of sunlight. Imagine a reef reaching down to the very depths of the ocean and facing, say, east. From early sunrise until the sun has passed its zenith, this reef would be bathed in life-giving sunlight. From that moment onwards, the west side of the reef gets its share of the sunlight until dusk. In the Blue Hole, this deep tube in the middle of a sandy reef, the opposite side of the hole would surely act to block out the sun until much later in the day, probably reducing the amount of available sunlight in any one day by over half.

It was interesting to note that after a dive in the Blue Hole most of the divers put it down as 'interesting', but would now prefer to dive elsewhere on the reef.

We left Half Moon Cay on the Monday morning. It was a clear bright day and we planned to dive from the landing craft as we passed over the reef. As the last divers were being recovered, a storm blew up and we were back into foul seas and a rough trip home. The four days were, however, extremely useful as I was already planning to spend two weeks on that particular Cay.

● *Above*: Hawksbill Turtle—the most elusive and shy of all the large creatures we saw.

● There is a total of over 200 miles of reef in Belize and wherever the divers choose to descend they are confronted with exciting forms of marine life. The visiting diver is never disappointed.

● Five divers from
my own diving club
during a routine dive
on Gallows Point
Reef.

● *Below*: Easter 1988.
Nine divers from
'Reef Roamer II'
enjoying the delights
of a reef dive led by
Michael the boat's
skipper.

Exercise 'Manta Ray'

During February we chartered a dive boat, a converted shrimp trawler called 'Reef Roamer II', from 'Out Island Divers' of San Pedro. There were 12 divers in the party, including 10 who had learned to dive during the previous three months and George Phillips, a professional diving instructor who had only arrived from England the previous day and had been given no chance to get jet-lagged, let alone recover from it.

We departed from Belize City at 7 am and, after a brief stop at San Pedro, sailed for Mexican waters. When travelling to a foreign country by boat you must first visit a recognised port of entry. This was to be Xcalak (pronounced Ischcalak) a small village that was decimated by a hurricane in the fifties and has never recovered from the shock. Over 3,500 people lived in Xcalak before that storm and it was an important copra producing region, well supplied with roads and a communication network essential to any industrial area.

It took a full day to get to Xcalak, where we stayed overnight before departing for the reef at first light. A quick glance at chart 1220 'Gulf of Honduras and Yucatan Channel' will give a good idea of the diving conditions to be found in this part of the world. However, one reef, just to the north of Belize, will immediately catch the eye; the reef in question is called Banco Chinchorro and that was where we were headed.

We needed extensive permits for this trip. Being soldiers we required political clearance—which only just arrived in time. We then required permission to dive the Chinchorro, an area of archaeological importance protected by Mexican law. This is a most sensible approach to protecting an important part of Mexico's heritage.

Wrecks have been running aground on the Chinchorro since Man first made some form of rude craft and went to sea. Many modern steel wrecks are evident, but a number of Spanish Galleons have also been found and partially excavated. One particular site harboured over 40 cannon, until an enterprising individual decided to remove them all for himself. He was later discovered and arrested.

We were allowed to dive the reef as long as we observed a number of conditions. We were not allowed to touch or remove any wreckage, or Black Coral; we also had to pay for a local guide called Eloy to accompany the trip. We, ourselves, were more than happy to observe all of these rules since we only wanted to take photographs. However, the guide did cost us a lot of extra cash and this was paid on the understanding that he knew exactly where to find the wrecks we were seeking.

We formed ourselves into two teams; George led one and I led the other. The diving plan remained the same throughout this brief but eventful trip: when one team was in the water, the other remained on the surface at any one time. This worked very well. The first wreck we were shown was well inside the reef in less than 10 feet of water. Lying on the sand was a single piece of rotten wood about 15 feet long—this was described as a Spanish Galleon and I was not impressed! I can understand the excitement of excavating such a wreck, perhaps reconstructing the remaining timbers and displaying all the artefacts discovered. However, we were not allowed to touch anything, and a single piece of wood in shallow water was not what we came for. Back on board 'Reef Roamer' we opted for a reef dive to 30 metres to round-off the day.

I explained carefully to our guide exactly what I was looking for and we began our second day on a steel wreck. We were again inside the reef and, at 20 feet, I still considered it a shallow dive. I was beginning to wonder whether our problem was a communication gap or a distinct lack of knowledge on the part of Ilois. His idea of wreck-diving was completely different from my own. I was looking for intact or semi-intact steel ships underwater, at a reasonable depth. There were certainly plenty of such ships up on top of the reef.

During the month before the trip commenced, everyone I had spoken to with knowledge of the Chinchorro could describe the wrecks we had come to see. In one place, I was told, there are three steel ships sitting one on top of the other: in other places the ships are upright on the seabed and completely intact. If only one of those people had been our guide. My mind went back to the Maiden Islands off the coast of Ulster; how spectacular those wrecks would be if the waters of the Irish Sea were as clear as those of the Caribbean.

At the end of the second day of our expedition, to our great disappointment, we realised that our guide did not know the whereabouts of any large steel wrecks. For the remainder of the expedition, we decided where we wanted to dive. There were lots of clues as to where ships might founder. Prevailing tides and winds were considered, but, before we begin to sound too expert, the biggest clue of all was wreckage protruding from the sea's surface. We commenced by diving right next to an old steel hulk. This ship had been a large tramp steamer with the bridge 'amidships': both the stern section and the bow section were missing, leaving the centre of the ship, complete with bridge, high and dry on the reef looking like a North Sea oil rig. It was the missing sections that we sought underwater. Apparently this particular hulk was a classic case of insurance 'write-off'. Local fishermen had watched as the ship sailed close to the reef, it then turned and headed out to sea for about five miles before turning once again, making straight for the reef at full speed. This all happened 17 years ago and the ship has been broken up over successive winter storms. We found very little wreckage underwater and it is likely that any large parts ripped off by a storm had floated right over the 'drop-off' and were now resting in very deep water.

However, on the way to this wreck, we did pass a mast sticking up out of the water. On most sea-going craft, the mast is set firmly right through the vessel and secured to the keel itself. It therefore did not require a degree in maritime architecture to realise that underneath that mast we would find a ship—we did. Large pieces of wreckage were spread over a considerable area. We found the anchors and chains, brass fittings, the engine room and all the paraphernalia one would associate with a wreck that has never been salvaged or even dived before. Certainly, several years of winter storms and rough seas had taken their toll, but nothing else had interfered with this ship.

● Exercise Manta Ray and the divers amongst the wreckage of a ship that we found by ourselves. Although well broken up the wreck was unsalvaged and—before our visit—undived.

● Grey Angelfish. These and other Angels were very common. One group of divers were successful in hand feeding a number of these fish. The fish remembered this and looked to the divers for more food on each successive dive.

● *Below*: An example of the 'drop off' that can be found anywhere on the reefs of Belize. The coral seems to go on forever although it is always more prolific in the shallower water.

Wrecks all over the world act like a magnet to fish and this particular wreck was no exception. The sheer abundance and variety of fish life added another dimension to the diving. We also witnessed a strange feeding phenomenon that I have never seen before and the spectacle had me spellbound. Our wreck had struck close to two offshoots of reef; one of these reached out to the left at about an angle of 45 degrees and the other off to the right at about the same angle. This created a perfectly natural 'V' shaped fish trap. Seven very large Jewfish (a grouper-like fish) were herding a large shoal—possibly over 5000 fish—of small silvery Blue Runners into this 'trap'. The Jewfish were spaced about four to five metres apart covering the large exit from the trap. As each of the big fish took its turn to feed on the milling shoal, the remainder of the group would move position and keep the shoal within the trap. There may have been no communication audible to the human ear, but the communication between those fish was certainly present. It was as though one of these large creatures was directing which one of their number was next in turn to feed. Unfortunately our presence brought the proceedings to an early conclusion.

The remaining dives on the voyage were spent on this particular wreck. It was not quite what we had come to see, but we had a most satisfying series of dives on a wreck which had saved the trip from complete failure. After the last of the dives on the fourth day, we set sail once again for Xcalak and arrived at 5 pm.

At Xcalak, we were told that the Port Captain would not process the ship's papers until 9 am the following morning, but we needed to leave by 6 am in order to get to Belize before dark. However, we found the Port Captain's charming secretary and she was most helpful in obtaining our papers from him and processing them. But our problems were not over yet. Just as soon as we were all back on board, the Captain went to the local military commander and ordered the boat searched for contraband from the Chinchorro Reef. My divers are a disciplined bunch and we hadn't broken any laws—we hadn't even collected a single sea-shell. The Mexican Marines searched the ship and apologised, explaining that they were only doing their duty: they each left with a can of cold beer from fellow soldiers.

Chinchorro is another atoll reef. As such it is as colourful and exciting as any of the reefs found in this corner of the globe. It would therefore be wrong to paint a depressing picture simply because we did not find what we were promised. The wrecks are there and people do know exactly how to find them—we were simply unlucky. However, I do believe that the potential exists at Chinchorro to create one of the foremost underwater centres of the world.

Over 40 years after the end of World War II, the authorities in such countries as Guam in the south Pacific are trying to preserve and protect what is left of the war-time wrecks that have been plundered in the intervening years. In Chinchorro that protection already exists. The pioneer spirit is still strong in the human race and divers will travel a long way to visit a new dive-site; an intact ship, a new wreck on the diving map of the world and people will flock to see it and photograph it. Chinchorro has trememdous potential and, if it should ever become a world-class diving location, Xcalak could well rise and become an important tourist resort.

Storm at sea

Maintaining my links with 'Out Island Divers', my good friend George Phillips and I booked ourselves on one of their two-day trips. 'Reef Roamer' is notorious for its consistent late starts and this trip was no exception. Apart from George and myself, there were eight couples on board, all of whom were looking forward to diving the Blue Hole. On this trip I was 'off-duty' and therefore not fettered by the 30 metre depth restriction. I had every intention of seeing the Blue Hole in all its splendour.

We left San Pedro about one and a half hours late. As we had been told to be on board before 6 am, most people were complaining of missed sleep. There is a sign at San Pedro air-port which reads 'Welcome to San Pedro where you will not be a stranger for long'. It is very true—in San Pedro nobody is a stranger for very long and the 10 divers on board 'Reef Roamer' soon became friends.

Yet again the weather was poor and the sea quite choppy. At times the swell was as much as two metres, which made life uncomfortable for most of us. Nevertheless, we crossed to the north of Turneffe Island and we were diving by mid-day. After the dive, we anchored inside the reef where the water was calm and had a light lunch. I found myself telling my companions all about the Blue Hole and Lighthouse Reef. Having just spent six

● Trunkfish.

● *Below*: Steve Thayer enjoys a joke across the meal table during exercise Lone Shark on Half Moon Cay.

days on board this very boat, I told them all about 'Reef Roamer' and Michael the Skipper, in whom, incidentally, I had complete faith. The weather was undoubtedly worsening but we set sail for Lighthouse Reef just the same.

The distance was 20 nautical miles from the north of Turneffe to a point just north of Long Cay where we could get inside the reef and find calm water. On a good day, the journey would have taken no more than two and a half hours. Instead, what followed was almost six hours of never-ending torture. The sky darkened and the sea boiled. Occasionally we hit a large wave head-on and the force of the water invariably pounded the doors to the cabin like a battering-ram and blew them wide-open.

● A group of divers about to submerge during exercise Lone Shark.

● *Below*: A broken wreck five miles north of Half Moon Cay. The Blue Hole lies on a course of 330 degrees from this wreck.

At no time did Michael discuss matters with the passengers, nor did he even consider turning around and making for the calm waters inside the reef at Turneffe. One young lady seemed to spend the entire trip over the stern of the boat. I was concerned that she could easily be lost overboard and hated to think how we would recover someone in these seas. Her name was Sarah and I sat down with her at the stern of the ship and offered what comforting words I could. Meanwhile Susan sat at the table with her head resting on top of her folded arms. I thought she was sleeping through the commotion until, after above five hours, I noticed that she was soaked. It was neither the sea nor the rain that had left her in such a state; absolutely terrified, she had been sweating profusely for the last five hours.

Pam did manage to sleep through most of it. That is until a particularly nasty wave sent her flying across the deck. Her reflexes were quite amazing—one minute she was asleep and the next, violently ejected from the bench seat. She automatically rolled right over as she crossed the open deck and landed perfectly, in a sitting position, on the bench opposite.

I made the awkward journey forward to the wheelhouse on several occasions. At the height of the storm, we were in the middle of the sea and it was the same distance to continue with our trip as it was to return home. Michael was searching the horizon for sight of land. A large hatch had fallen across his big toe, he was limping badly and had bled all over the wheelhouse floor but managed to tie a piece of oily rag around the wound. Because of his injury, it was I who made the journey to the upper deck and climbed the mast. If I had thought the ship was swaying down below, that feeling was nothing compared to the sensation as I went up the slippery mast. I had recently injured my own shoulder and I progressed quite slowly, moving only one hand or one foot at a time.

Clinging precariously to the top of the mast, I scanned the horizon for some time and I remember thinking "Middleton, what the hell are you doing up here in a gale?" Then I saw it—as we reached the peak of each successive jarring wave I had a brief glimpse of a distant island. I called down but no-one could hear me in the violent wind. Carefully making my way to the wheelhouse, I gave the passengers the good news as I went through the cabin.

A study of the chart of Lighthouse Reef will show that the

only entrances through the reef on the western shore are just to
the north of Long Cay. We were convinced that we were looking at Long Cay in the distance and, with the wind from the
north, we had two options. We could either turn due north and
head directly into the storm before turning into the reef or we
could turn south and travel with the waves, a journey which
would be much easier on both boat and passengers, and enter
the reef just to the west of Half Moon Cay. With two hours of
daylight left to find sheltered water, Michael opted for the
northern route.

After a full hour of battling against those horrendous seas,
we realised to our horror that the island was not Long Cay but
Northern Cay! With only one hour of daylight left, we were in
trouble. There is a gap through the reef on the northern tip, but
nobody would risk such a perilous passage in the face of a
howling gale. We did try to raise the northern lighthouse-
keeper, but he was not aware of our plight and was not listening to his radio. With daylight quickly fading, we turned south
and began to run with the storm. Michael searched the reef for
a gap and, on his second attempt, he found one. We were inside
the reef and looking for a safe anchorage with less than 20
minutes of daylight left. Running aground on soft mud, we
reversed off again quite easily before finding the anchorage
that gave everyone a much-welcomed, peaceful night.

I have mentioned before that the weather in this area of
the world is fickle. The following morning was bright, clear and
calm without a single cloud in the sky. Everyone was well-
rested and looking forward to the Blue Hole. Sailing very carefully between the jagged outcrops of coral within the reef, we
arrived inside the Blue Hole at 10 am and we were diving
within 30 minutes of our arrival.

Some of the divers had never been very deep before, so I
explained the symptoms of nitrogen narcosis—the euphoric
effects of pressure associated with deep-diving. Michael was
also the dive-leader, although he had no formal qualifications.
His pre-dive briefing was quite inadequate, so George and I
filled in the gaps and promised to 'bring up the rear' and look
after any stragglers.

It was a tremendous dive. We found the famous ledge about
which I had read and heard so much. The bottom of this perfectly flat ledge is 50 metres (165 feet) from the surface and it
cuts back into the rock some 15 to 20 feet, creating a long

● When stalactites and stalagmites meet they form a column like this one found at 50 metres (165 feet) down inside the Blue Hole.

ever-narrowing cavern until the roof reaches the floor right at the back. Here were the stalactites, stalagmites and columns that do not exist in the shallower waters of the Blue Hole. It was indescribable: where else in the world can you see this kind of phenomenon, every exciting facet well lit by the sunlight far above? Yet again, I was seeing something fascinating underwater for the very first time. This was different from Ben's Cave in the Bahamas, yet equally as magnificent; a 'V'-shaped ledge cut into solid limestone with massive dark icicles hanging from the ceiling. It was as though the entire journey had been worth all the suffering just for this one dive. All too soon the dive was over and we proceeded towards the surface for decompression.

After breakfast, we left Lighthouse Reef and headed back to Turneffe for one more dive before arriving back at San Pedro just as it was getting dark. We all had dinner together that evening in a hotel on the island: 10 new friends with a shared experience that brought us closer together.

● Kevin Carter—a Marine amongst Paras—my Diving Officer on Half Moon Cay about to lead yet another exciting dive.

● *Below*: My diving partner above the reef and 'drop-off'.

Exercise 'Lone Shark'

The Caribbean is the only sea in the world where I have seen large 'intact' ships high and dry up on the reef. We saw them in the Bahamas, Turks and Caicos islands and, as I have just described, in Mexico. Within a few miles of Half Moon Cay, there are four virtually intact wrecks and a further two well broken-up. It is ironic that these countries, which depend so much on tourism for foreign income, actually need those ships to be underwater in order to attract the visiting diver.

'Lone Shark', a two week project involving 22 divers, commenced in early March. Once again, we were based at Half Moon Cay and, on this occasion, we had closed down the training facility at Hunting Cay and brought all available equipment and boats with us. Since my trip to the Blue Hole on 'Reef Roamer' I had not been idle. I desperately wanted to show my divers what I had seen and I tried several ways to get around the 30 metre limit. Unfortunately, it was rather late in the day when I discovered how to do it. Let me explain why the limit has been imposed.

Royal Navy rules dictate that diving must be limited to 30 metres if there is no recompression facility within four hours travel. This rule only applies to diving on duty. However, getting to a chamber is not that simple. A diver suffering from the effects of decompression sickness, caused by a too rapid ascent from deep water, will find the situation made a lot worse if he were to take to the air and simply fly to Miami. As the aircraft gains height, the pressure will drop even further, ex-acerbating the diver's condition. An American organisation called the Diving Alert Network, DAN for short, operates a small fleet of air ambulances, pressurised to maintain surface pressure throughout the voyage. Unfortunately these small jets are based in the USA and would have to travel to Belize before the victim could make the two hour journey to the recompression facility in Miami. For many years British service diving clubs on worldwide expeditions have dived regularly to depths of 45 metres (150 feet) without this restriction being imposed. Their safety record, which is one of the finest records of any of the adventurous sports, has always rested on the first class training syllabus of the British Sub-Aqua Club, followed by sound dive-planning and the safe execution of those plans.

Amateur divers get into difficulties, often with tragic results, when they attempt to take on underwater tasks beyond their capabilities. In the same way professional divers have been known to get into trouble when trying out sports diving equipment that is unfamiliar to them. The best person to tackle a professional job of work underwater is a professional diver. Similarly, the best person to take charge of a group of amateur sports divers is a qualified sports diving instructor. It therefore seem iniquitous to me that the professional divers of the Royal Navy should be able to dictate the rules for sports diving to all three services, especially as the Army and RAF have far more sports divers and diving clubs than the Navy. I wish they would put their petty jealousies to one side and help to put the word 'adventure' back into adventure sports.

Anyway, as I said, I had not been idle, I had discovered the existence of at least two recompression chambers in Cozumel. A friend of mine in the RAF estimated that, if we had an accident on Half Moon Cay, it would take one hour to bring the victim back to Belize and a further 90 minutes to fly to Cozumel. Even allowing for delays, this was well inside four hours. However the aircraft would be a military PUMA transport helicopter and no country likes to see foreign military aircraft over its airspace. We applied for political clearance, but the application got bogged down and there was insufficient time for this approach to succeed. The diving therefore remained at the stated limit of 30 metres and a great opportunity for adventurous diving was lost forever.

In contrast, the weather was excellent. We completed over 500 man dives and dived over 60 completely different sites. Even on those days when it was windy, we were always able to find a sheltered spot. On this particular trip we were expecting to see some of the ocean's largest creatures and I had my cameras along on every dive. During the first week, we were diving to 24 metres (80 feet) and by the end of that particular dive I had finished the roll of film in my camera, just as we arrived back at the anchor. I was about to give the signal to surface, when along came an amazing creature—an albino Manta Ray—and I did not have a single frame left inside the camera. My diving partners were slow in letting me forget that one.

At the end of the first week two army Gazelle helicopters arrived, granting us 30 minutes flying time to photograph the reef from the air. We concentrated on the Blue Hole, firstly with our boats in the water and then with the second Gazelle in the frame. In the space of those 30 minutes, I exposed seven rolls of film.

● Author at the controls of his 18 foot dory 'Sub Mariner'.

● *Left*: Aerial views of the famous Blue Hole.

● Less than 100 metres from the shores of Half Moon Cay the wreck of the Elksund high and dry on the reef. How much more spectacular this wreck would have been if it were underwater.

● *Below*: The Blue Hole, though easily seen from the air, cannot be seen at sea level until one is inside it. This wreck is five miles north of Half Moon Cay and an essential landmark in finding the Blue Hole.

The one creature sadly lacking during the trip was a shark. Even Nurse Shark, which had always been very common, were totally absent. Despite all our efforts we could not lure the Hammerhead out of the Blue Hole and elsewhere, on all parts of this large reef, we saw no sharks at all. Many of the divers had come hoping to see a shark, so I set about trying to find one. Each day the local fisherman cleaned their catch before placing the fish on blocks of ice for transport to Belize City. They very kindly put all the blood and guts into a large bin and each afternoon I took this out to the reef. We threw this gunge into the water and waited about 30 minutes before diving, but to no avail. At first sight this behaviour may seem a dangerous practice, but it was quite safe. The divers were not jumping in amongst the blood and there was no food in the water. I had learned a lot from George Friese in the Bahamas and I was trying to pass on a little of this knowledge. With the absence of sharks, I failed to provide anything. One afternoon, a group declined to dive with me saying they would prefer a long shallow dive on top of the reef. I was still looking for sharks, so I took some more divers in the opposite direction—the group in the shallow water saw the Hammerhead!

Divers who swim well above the reef present a profile similar to that of a predator and consequently frighten the fish. I instructed each group accompanying me to keep as low as possible over the reef: this strategy paid off towards the end of the expedition, when I spotted a turtle in the distance. It was too far away for a photograph, so all we could do was hug the reef and wait patiently. All the divers did as I asked and the turtle turned and swam straight towards us. I waited for the right moment to take the first photograph, thinking that the flash would quickly frighten the creature, but it was not alarmed by the light and, after two photographs, it was still heading straight towards us. As it passed by, I turned the camera and caught it on a piece of coral. The noise startled the turtle and it disappeared straight down the 'drop-off' at tremendous speed!

All the divers were upgraded to the next diving qualification and most achieved 25 quite exciting dives. Even the chef had a go and managed four dives in between working very hard indeed. The landing-craft arrived on the Tuesday and, because it was so warm, we dismantled the tents and decided to sleep in the open for one night in order to make a very early start on the following morning. The weather had been excellent, but on the one night when we had no tents it rained furiously making our last night on Half Moon Cay most uncomfortable.

As soon as we returned to Airport Camp, all the kit and equipment had to be packed ready for the return to UK. Exercise 'Lone Shark' brought the diving to a close and it was good to finish on a high note. We had made the most of our tour in Belize and all the divers can feel quite satisfied with the part they played in making it such a success. We had explored the vast and unspoilt wonders of the barrier reef as an organised and disciplined group paying attention, at all times, to the rules and regulations designed to conserve this marvellous underwater world.

POSTSCRIPT

So there it is, a record of the adventures of an amateur diver, covering slightly more than the 10 years indicated by the title, and taking in 900 dives. For the future, there are a number of projects I hope to get involved in, although my one over-riding ambition is to become a BSAC National Instructor. If there is one single message emanating from this book , I hope it is the importance of sound basic training. This training continues long after those first dives in open water and long after those first diving qualifications have been achieved. The BSAC will ensure that your training is both thorough and complete. Offices of the British Sub-Aqua Club can be found at: 16 Upper Woburn Place, London, WC1H OQW. Be careful down there!

LIST OF DIVERS WHO PARTICIPATED IN PHASE 1 OF OPERATION RALEIGH

SWR STAFF

John Blashford-Snell	Commander
Ned Middleton	Chief Diver
Charles Hastie	Diving Assistant
Eric Niemi	Diving Assistant
Alan Westcobb	OIC Barbary Beach
Barry Moss	OIC Turks & Caicos
David Whittaker	Adjutant
Nick Horne	Ops Officer
David Burden	Communications
Susie Long-Innes	PRO
Jane Dunbar	Doctor
David Allfrey	Recce Group
Gordon Wilson	Chef
Bob Estridge	Communications Assistant
Sarah McDermot	Secretary
David Cross	SWR 2nd Officer
Caroline Ashe	Scientist
Val Snewin	Scientist
Simon Leafe	Sponsorship Co-Ordinator
Mitch Mitchell	OIC Small Boats
David Hughes	Diving Officer
Fiona Dolman	Diving Officer
Steve Hubbard	Diving Officer
Les Holliday	Diving Officer
Rob Palmer	Cave Diving Group

SUMMARY

United Kingdom	144
Canada	16
Australia	14
America	11
Japan	6
New Zealand	5
Bahamas	4
Channel Islands	4
Turks & Caicos	2
Hong Kong	1
Malaysia	1
Oman	1
Venezuela	1
TOTAL	210

CANADA
Robert Aubrey
Dave Beaulieu
Don Bobbiwash
Ray Boyle
Dave Brown
Robin Cass
Crane Gittens
Bob Kay
Rick Mason
Joe MacInness
Rob Proctor
Errol Sharpkaya
Jerry Shaw
Justin Taylor
Stewart Waldeck
Lisa Walker

AUSTRALIA
Sue Benson
Scott Brown
Ross Clifford
Nick Findley
Louise Grandfield
Rob McIntyre
John McKinley
Ashley McKinnon
Mark Parssey
Sam Pearce
Mike Rice
Jenny Sheenan
James Whitworth
Mark Woods

USA
Katrina Abbot
Chris Benson
Mark Benson
Dorian Carroll
Jenny Grainger
Sharon King
Lissette Lecat
James Moore
Lisa Paea
Diane Rosenthal
Anitra Thorharg

TURKS & CAICOS
Andy Williams
Wendel Williams

JAPAN
Kaori Hashimoto
Omata Hiroasu
Kazuhide Horriachi
Nori Omi
Tadaki Togami
Hyjimia Tozaki

NEW ZEALAND
Chris Easton
Graeme Espin
Jeff Larsen
Denise Maskill
Carey Mills

CHANNEL ISLANDS
Heather Allen
Jason De Carteret
Peter Hearne
Andre Rabat

VENEZUELA
Elvir MacDonald

OMAN
Abdulla al Baluchi

BAHAMAS
Jason Burrows
George Friese
Bob Montpetit
Delbert Smith

MALAYSIA
Razak

HONG KONG
Lui Ho Wong

UNITED KINGDOM
Helen Adams
Samantha Adlam
Tim Ainstree
Pete Alger
Lucy Anderson
Jo Baker
Liz Baker
Mark Bakewell
Michael Barton
Christine Bell
John Bergin
John Berry
Helen Bird
Victoria Blashford-Snell
Lisa Bond
Rob Brister
Nick Brooks
David Bryant
Paul Burrows
Clive Bush
Andy Callaghan
Fiona Campbell
David Chinn
John Cole
Adam Colwood
Richard Cook
Jackie Cotton
Vicky Crawley
Lloyd Davies
Paul Dumont
Ian Dunn
John Feetenby
Warren Flavell
Paul Fogarty
Ian Fox
Simon Frame
Richard Gibson
Jim Giles
Isobel Gillies
Katy Gray
Margaret Hall
Diarmuid Hanley
Robert Hardingham
Gary Hardington
Farlan Harris
Bob Hartlebury
John Hately
Pete Hatt
Jenny Hayes
Martin Haynes

Chris Henry
Max Hislop
Martha Holmes
Richard Horner
Roy Jarvis
Amanda Jenkins
Phil Jones
Kester Keighley
Robin Kelk
Chris Kendall
Nigel Kennet
Trevor Kimber
David King
Andy Long
Ian Lott
John Louch
Karen Lyppiat
Murdo MacDonald
Paul Machell
Tim Makin
Karen Malloy
Mike Marr
Ian Marshall

Andy Martin
Morag Maxwell
Russell Maylin
Maura McEwan
Trevor Morris
Jim Noonan
Claire Norris
John Norris
Jo Norrsworthy
Jane Orr-Ewing
Mark Palmer
Huw Parker
Russell Powell
Paul Power
Godfrey Priest
Tom Pringle
Trevor Rees
Marie Reid
Julia Richards
Phil Richards
Martin Roberts
Kevin Robinson
Pete Seymour

Ian Shaw
Paul Sheridan
Allison Smith
Phil Smith
Mary Stafford-Smith
Kevin Thomas
Steve Thomas
Phil Tong
Sally Toye
Karen Travers
Robert Trott
Mark Vinal
Gordom Wallace
Duncan Walpole
Phil Wells
Matt Weston
Shirley Whiteside
Dave Whiting
Angela Wilkinson
Nicki Wilkinson
Andrew Williams
Keith Williams
Paul Williams

1. NIKON F2A

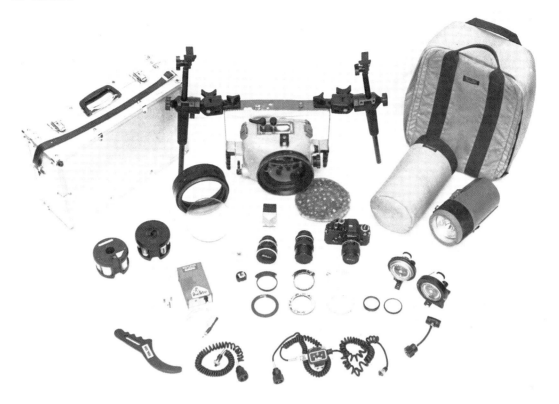

1. Camera case.
2. Camera housing case.
3. 'Sea and Sea' aluminium underwater camera housing fitted with dome part for wide angle lens.
4. Flat port for narrow angle lens (with extension tubes).
5. Port cover.
6. Ikelite flash brackets.
7. Nikon F2A 35mm camera (fitted with 55mm micro lens).
8. Nikon 135mm lens.
9. Nikon 20mm wide angle lens.
10. Nikon Action Finder—This replaces standard camera view finder for use in underwater camera housing.
11. Camera retaining screw.
12. Camera hot shoe flash adaptor.
13. Lens aperture and focusing gears.
14. Lens filters.
15. Ikelite Substrobe 150 —Underwater flashgun.
16. Carrying case for Substrobe 150.
17. Powerpack for Substrobe 150—Exchangeable batteries.
18. Powerpack for Substrobe 150—Rechargeable.
19. Recharging unit.
20. Port securing wrench.
21. Non automatic flash lead.
22. Automatic flash sensor and lead.
23. 'T' piece for connecting flashguns.
24. Two Sekonic underwater light metres.

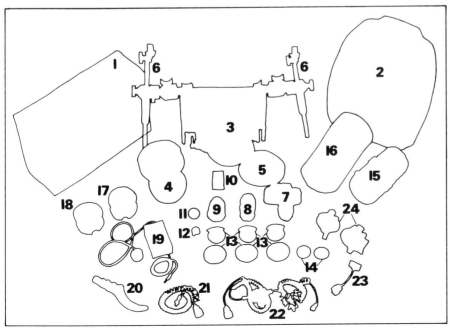

2. NIKONOS V

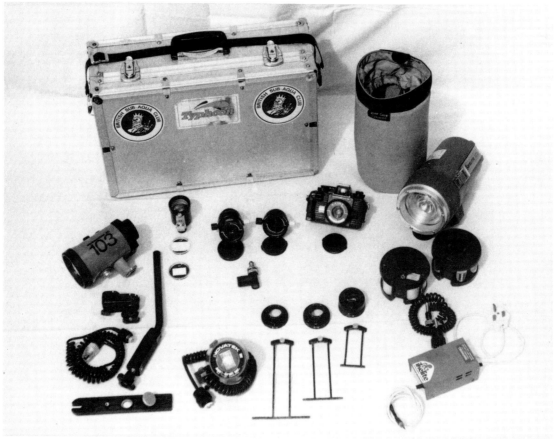

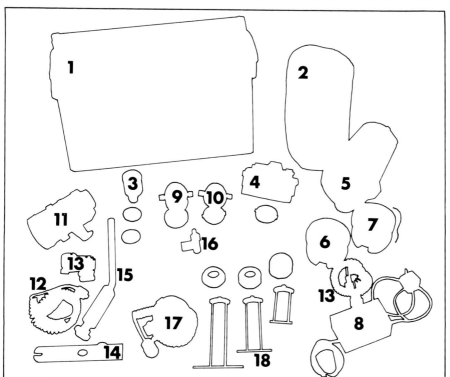

1. Camera case.
2. Strobe carrying bag.
3. Viewfinder with fittings for each lens.
4. Nikonos V camera (fitted with 35mm lens).
5. Ikelite Substrobe 150.
6. Rechargeable power pack for Ikelite strobe.
7. Alternative battery power pack.
8. Recharging unit.
9. Nikonos 80mm lens and lens cap.
10. Nikonos 28mm lens and lens cap.
11. Nikonos SB 103 strobe.
12. Strobe lead.
13. Adjustable strobe attaching unit.
14. Camera and strobe base plate.
15. Strobe arm.
16. Conversion plug —Nikonos to Ikelite.
17. Novatek III strobe.
18. Extension tubes and frame finders.

THE COMPLETE UNIT
COMPRISING BOTH CAMERAS.

All my personal photographic equipment was purchased from
'Greenaway Marine' of Swindon.   I chose this firm because they
are a small, but expanding family business who take a great deal of
trouble in looking after the customer. No job is ever too small and
their invaluable advice is free.

CREDITS.

CHAPTER EIGHT: Line Drawing: HMS Drake courtesy 'Conway's All the World's
Fighting Ships 1860–1905'.
Photo: Georgetown Victory—Unknown source, although this pic-
ture also appears in 'Shipwrecks of the Ulster Coast'.

CHAPTER TEN: Photo: Chief Diver with diving equipment by Chris
Sainsbury/ORPIX.
Photo: Cave diver by Mark Vinall/ORPIX.

THE REMAINING PHOTOGRAPHS WERE TAKEN BY THE AUTHOR.

BIBLIOGRAPHY.

Sport Diving — The BSAC Diving Manual.
Shipwrecks of the Ulster Coast — Ian Wilson.
Fishes of the Sea — John and Gillian Lythgoe.
Conway's All the World's Fighting Ships 1860–1905.
Marine Life — David & Jennifer George.
Hamlyn Guide to Shells of the World.
Operation Raleigh — John Blashford Snell.
Galápagos — Titicaca — The Blue Holes; Three
Adventures— —Jacques-Yves Cousteau and Philippe
Diolé.

PERSONAL DIVING STATISTICS

Down To	Europe Freshwater	British Isles	Holland	Italy	Norway	Hong Kong
10 m	17	82	1	3	6	65
20 m	37	76	5	5	19	94
30 m	8	25	5	2	6	
40 m	2	10	1	7	2	
50 m				8		
60 m				6		
70 m				4		
Totals	64	193	12	35	33	167